MALCOLM

BEYOND THE WIRE

A True Story of Allied POWs in Italy 1943-1945

WORLD WAR II ESCAPE AND EVASION

EMILIA PUBLISHING

First published in Great Britain in 2009 by
EMILIA PUBLISHING
Woodlands, Bryn Gardens, Newtown,
Powys, SY16 2DR, United Kingdom
www.emiliapublishing.com

A CIP Catalogue of this book is available from
the British Library

ISBN: 978-0-9538964-5-5

Cover designed and typeset in Plantin 10½pt
by Chandler Book Design
www.chandlerbookdesign.co.uk

Printed in Great Britain by
the MPG Books Group, Bodmin and King's Lynn

Contents

ALSO BY MALCOLM TUDOR

*At War in Italy 1943-1945, True Adventures
in Enemy Territory.*

*British Prisoners of War in Italy:
Paths to Freedom.*

*Escape from Italy 1943-45, Allied Escapers
and Helpers in Fascist Italy.*

*Prisoners and Partisans: Escape and Evasion
in World War II Italy.*

*Special Force: SOE and the
Italian Resistance 1943-1945.*

The books can be ordered:

Online at www.emiliapublishing.com
Or from UK and internet booksellers

ACKNOWLEDGEMENTS

I would like to thank the former prisoners of war in
Italy, the Italians, and their relatives, who have provided
me with information.

Special thanks to Doctor Oreste Scaglioni for also writing the
Foreword, and to Eileen for her general advice.

One photograph kindly contributed by John Langrishe
and another by Monica Woosnam. The other images are
from my collection.

I have translated any items in Italian.

Foreword

By Doctor Oreste Scaglioni
Wartime partisan officer

I feel very honoured to be invited by Malcolm to introduce this new book, which replaces his earlier title, *British Prisoners of War in Italy: Paths to Freedom*, in view of information gathered over the past nine years.

As a partisan of the Val d'Arda formation of Piacenza in the years 1943-1945, I was in contact with a group of 20 British ex-prisoners of war. They had escaped from the camp at Fontanellato (Parma) on 9 September 1943 and taken refuge in the Trinità area.

I spent several months of partisan life in the valley with a number of the ex-prisoners during 1943 and 1944. In particular, we survived the German roundup of July 1944 together.

From that time I still have the vivid memory of the contribution made by Malcolm's mother, Mrs Clara Elvira Maria Tudor, born Dall' Arda, who with complete disregard for the danger provided assistance to the ex-prisoners. This was carried out through the tiring journeys she made every day on foot from Castell' Arquato to Trinità with a heavy knapsack of food supplies, clothing, medicines, and maps of the zone.

Malcolm has kindly recognised and described in his books the help given in those years by the families and partisans of the Piacentine valleys to the British ex-prisoners who had escaped from camps in the Parma and Piacenza areas.

Therefore, sincere thanks for this welcome testimony, which so honours us, and a fervent wish for the success of the new book.

Glossary

A FORCE: Allied deception and escape organisation.

AFHQ: Allied Force Headquarters, Mediterranean.

ALEXANDER CERTIFICATE: Document awarded to Italians who assisted Allied personnel behind enemy lines following the armistice with Italy on 3 September 1943.

ALLIED SCREENING COMMISSION: The awards bureau.

ESCAPE: To break free from confinement in a prisoner of war camp or enemy country. Escaper = noun.

EVADE: To avoid or escape capture in enemy territory. Evader = noun. Most evaders in Italy were airmen.

GENEVA CONVENTION relative to the Treatment of Prisoners of War, 1929: International Humanitarian Law.

GREATER GERMANY: Germany and the states it annexed.

ICRC: International Committee of the Red Cross: The humanitarian agency with its HQ in Geneva, Switzerland.

IS 9: Cover name for MI 9 from 1944.

MI 9: British Military Intelligence, escape and evasion.

MIS-X: United States Military Intelligence Section, escape and evasion. X was often a code word for escape.

N SECTION: Escape and evasion section of A Force.

NO. 1 SPECIAL FORCE: Cover name for SOE in Italy.

PRISONER OF WAR (POW): A member of the armed services captured by the enemy in the course of military operations.

PROTECTING POWER: A neutral power that protects the interests of another in the territory of a third. In Italy, it was the USA until 11 December 1941, and Switzerland thereafter.

SPECIAL OPERATIONS EXECUTIVE (SOE): British secret service, subversion and sabotage against the enemy overseas.

SUCCESSFUL ESCAPE OR EVASION: When the serviceman joined his own forces, or those of an allied power, or had left the territory of the Detaining Power, or of an ally of the power.

1
Prisoners of War
in Italy

When the Allied invasion of the Italian mainland began on Friday, 3 September 1943, eighty thousand of their countrymen were already there as prisoners of war.

Italian figures in August disclosed that 75,533 enemy soldiers, sailors and airmen were held in the kingdom: 42,194 Britons, 26,126 from other Commonwealth countries, 9,903 European Allies - Free French, Greeks, Russians, and Yugoslavs - and 1,310 Americans. The total would have been increased by hundreds of men captured in ongoing operations.

A British War Office document circulated in the same month identified 52 main prisoner of war camps in Italy. There were also 18 prison hospitals and seven camps for civilian internees. The size and location of all but four of the hundreds of work camps for 'other ranks' were not known.[1]

The camps varied a great deal from site to site. Some were built to a standard plan, the familiar barracks-style huts, while others used existing buildings such as factories, hotels, large villas, castles, schools, colleges, and monasteries. POWs were taken from coastal transit camps to permanent prisons along the extensive rail network. By September 1943 some of the men had been captives for more than three years.

In the summer a brief message had been sent to the camps in

---

[1] The National Archives (hereafter TNA): Public Record Office (PRO) WO 224/178, POW Camps in Italy, List and Locations, August 1943.

Italy by coded letter or radio message. What became known as the War Office 'stand fast' order was dated 7 June. It was addressed to the Senior British Officer (SBO) or his Allied equivalent:

> *In the event of an Allied invasion of Italy, Officers Commanding prison camps will ensure that prisoners of war remain within camp. Authority is granted to all officers commanding to take necessary disciplinary action to prevent individual prisoners attempting to rejoin their own units.*

These plans did not take into consideration the possibility of German occupation. When this became a reality within hours of the announcement of Italian armistice and surrender on the evening of Wednesday, 8 September, every commander faced a dangerous dilemma. In the morning, they read out the 'stand fast' order to their men, but events were moving beyond their control. Instead of seeing advancing victorious Allied troops on the horizon, there were only Germans.

In the first three years of the war the Italians had proved to be skilful gaolers. Between December 1940 and July 1943 there were only 602 camp breakouts. Just six escapers managed to leave Italy and four of those went to the Vatican.

In contrast, following the Armistice of September 1943 almost 50,000 of the 80,000 prisoners of war were able to flee their camps. Though the majority were eventually recaptured and sent to prisons in Greater Germany, over 17,000 men retained their liberty.

An estimated 4,876 prisoners succeeded in escaping to neutral Switzerland, of whom 4,852 were from the Commonwealth and 24 from the United States. A further 12,828 servicemen crossed Allied lines within Italy (or were overrun by friendly forces), made up of 11,776 from the Commonwealth and 1,052 from the United States.

In addition, there were 2,815 evaders, mainly airmen, who had never been in enemy hands. Two hundred and sixty-seven reached Switzerland, of whom 64 were from the Commonwealth and 203 from the United States. Two thousand five hundred and forty-eight more evaders joined Allied forces within Italy, made up of 134 from the Commonwealth and 2,414 from the United States.[2]

Successful escape and evasion were in part the result of rescue work by the secret services: British MI 9 and United States MIS-X. In Italy they worked together under the banner of N Section of A Force, the deception and escape organisation of Allied Force Headquarters. The wartime head of MI 9, Brigadier Norman Crockatt, said that 33 per cent of global Commonwealth escapers and 90 per cent of evaders were brought out as a result of its organisation and activities.

Almost two thirds of the men who returned home were from Italy. After taking into account official rescue work, about two thirds of escapers and a tenth of evaders would have been saved, in British Prime Minister Winston Churchill's words, through 'the risks taken by members of the Italian Resistance and the simple people of the countryside.' As an escaper in South Africa during the Boer War, Churchill was all too aware that success depended on help from nationals of an enemy state.

On 11 July 1944 an Allied awards bureau for Italian helpers was set up in Rome. It was just five weeks and a day since the capital had been liberated. The war in the rest of Italy would continue for another 10 months.

The Allied Screening Commission (ASC) was part of A Force. The commission was 'responsible for giving recognition to, and compensating, persons in Italy who had assisted Allied personnel behind enemy lines following the Allied armistice with Italy on 3 September 1943.'

---

[2] TNA: PRO AIR 40/1897, Return of Escapers and Evaders up to 30 June 1945 by areas, services and nationalities.

The ASC was able to emerge so quickly because it took over the offices and staff of the remarkable British Organisation in Rome for Assisting Allied Escaped Prisoners of War. It succeeded in keeping 3,925 fugitive servicemen from 25 different countries out of the hands of the enemy.

As soon as arrangements had been made to repatriate the personnel, thoughts turned to the helpers. The military commander of the British Organisation, Major Sam Derry, spoke of 'a debt to those who risked everything to help us,' which was 'incalculable and perhaps never quite repayable.'

The diplomatic head of the escape line, Sir D'Arcy Osborne, British Minister to the Holy See, wrote in his final report in October 1944:

> *I take this opportunity to record my admiration for, and gratitude to the numberless Italians, mostly of the poorest peasant class in the country districts, who displayed boundless generosity and kindness to our men over a long and trying period. It must be remembered that in so doing, not only did they refuse the financial rewards for the denunciation of British prisoners of war which the Germans offered and which would have been a fortune to them, but they also showed magnificent abnegation and courage in sharing their few clothes and scanty food and, above all in risking their lives and the lives of their families and friends in disregarding the increasingly severe German injunctions against harbouring or helping British prisoners. A number of them indeed were shot by the Germans. We owe a debt to the Italian people in this respect that should not be forgotten and cannot be repaid.[3]*

---

[3] TNA: PRO WO 208/3396, Report on the activities of the British organisation in Rome.

The ASC's first commanding officer was William Simpson, a Glasgow Territorial gunner officer and former POW who had served as one of Major Derry's lieutenants. He was succeeded in October 1945 by Lieutenant Colonel Hugo de Burgh, who had been Senior British Officer at PG 49 Fontanellato.

To meet all the potential liabilities of the Allied Military Government, the ASC distributed claim forms to communes across Italy regarding 'Assistance Given to Allied Ex-Prisoners of War.' The completed forms were checked against the statements made by the servicemen to MI 9 and MIS-X. The top secret 'Appendix A' in the reports provided the names and addresses of the helpers, the nature of the assistance and the relevant dates.

The investigating officers summarised the claims under the headings of food and lodging, clothing, money, general unspecified assistance (GUA), and any damage to person or property. Each item was given a monetary value. There was no provision for rewarding risk, though in practice GUA was often used to cover activities such as carrying food and supplies to prisoners, or acting as a guide.

When all the forms had been processed, and the war had ended, formal award ceremonies were held across the peninsula. Italian speaking officers of the ASC expressed official thanks and awarded bilingual certificates of merit and cash reimbursements of expenses.

The ceremony in Rome in May 1946 honoured 700 guests. They had all sheltered Allied escapers and evaders during the nine months of German occupation. Another sizeable gathering was held in Milan. The Resistance escape line led by engineer Giuseppe Bacciagaluppi had carried 1,865 Allied escapers to Switzerland.

The certificates read:

This certificate is awarded to [hand-written name in stylised script] as a token of gratitude for and appreciation of the help given to the Sailors, Soldiers

*and Airmen of the British Commonwealth of Nations,
which enabled them to escape from, or evade capture
by the enemy.*

The documents bore the facsimile signature of Field Marshal HR Alexander, Supreme Allied Commander, Mediterranean Theatre. In 1946, when about to travel to Canada to become Governor General, he said:

Before leaving this Theatre, I would like to pay tribute to all those civilians who at one time or another voluntarily rendered, at considerable personal risk, very valuable assistance to Allied fugitive ex-prisoners of war and airmen, who were escaping from the enemy in German-occupied territory.

The gallant efforts of these countless helpers resulted in the safe and early return of thousands of our men to their homeland and families, and in many cases soon afterwards to further service with the armed forces. I know I am speaking on their behalf when I say they would all wish, if it were practicable, to thank their helpers personally and endeavour in some way to repay the debts which they have incurred. It is however my intention that due recognition be awarded and all material debts be repaid to every individual civilian who rendered assistance of whatever nature to Allied escapers. I am glad to say that this immense task is already in hand. It will of course take months to finish, but I give my assurance that everything will be done to see that no one is forgotten.

The Americans issued a similar certificate to their Italian helpers. The documents bore the signature of General Taggart McNarney, Commanding General of United States Armed Forces in the European Theatre of Operations.

Only one certificate was awarded per household. The actual number of helpers was far higher. In addition, as the head of the household was most likely to be a man, the contribution made by other family members often remained hidden.

William Simpson wrote that by the time the work of the ASC was completed in 1947, 'it had validated over 75,000 family claims of assistance to Allied escapers, with the presentation of official certificates and cash reimbursement.'

Another 25,000 claims were not acted upon. Some duplicated activities rewarded in the name of the head of the household, while others were incomplete, lacking in documentary evidence, or erroneous, though William Simpson, noted that 'false claims were rare.'

Recommendations made by the ASC for additional honours and awards to Italian civilians were blocked by the British Foreign Office in 1947. William Simpson recalled the reasons given for the decision: 'awards of decorations to Italians would give offence to British families bereaved at Italian hands, some might be Communists, and if some were awarded, reaction by others could be counter-productive.' In contrast, the United States awarded Italian nationals 17 Medals of Freedom, including three for outstanding service.

The Screening Commission was consolidated with its sister A Force organisation, IS 9, to form ASC (Italy) on 20 July 1945. Its work ended on 10 April 1947. The remaining functions were transferred to a new Prisoner of War Claims Commission, which was itself abolished on 31 October.

In 1948, ASC records were transferred to the United States at the request of General Eisenhower. They are still held by the National Archives and Records Administration (NARA) at College Park in Maryland.

For a generation after the war, official documents on escape and evasion were kept secret from the public on the grounds that the information they contained could still prove useful to an enemy. During this time, the story of survival and resistance in German-occupied Italy was largely revealed in POW autobiographies. The authors naturally emphasised the spontaneous generosity of the Italian civilians they met on their travels.

The official documents were finally declassified in the 1970s and 1980s. They included the individual helper files of the ASC in the United States, and the servicemen's escape and evasion reports at the United Kingdom National Archives at Kew. In addition, there are nominal lists of POWs, camp reports, liberation questionnaires, and recommendations for honours and awards.

My grandfather, Alfredo Dall' Arda, was one of the Italians presented with the Alexander Certificate. As with most recipients, assisting escaped prisoners of war was a collective effort, also involving my grandmother, Giuseppina, and my mother, Clara. They had returned to Italy in 1931 after running their restaurant in Upper James Street, Golden Square, London W1. My family owned a villa and a small hill farm in the medieval village of Castell' Arquato, Piacenza. The British and South African soldiers they helped came from officers' camp 49 Fontanellato in the adjoining province of Parma. The pretty village was the scene of the greatest escape in Italy. It is our destination in the next chapter.

2

The Camp

The most famous Italian camp for Allied prisoners of war was in the little Parmesan village of Fontanellato. The name means 'large fountain' and the commune is rich in underground springs and is bounded by two rivers, the Stirone and the Taro. The village is situated in the middle of the northern Italian plain, 110 kilometres south-east of Milan and 18 kilometres north-west of Parma, the provincial capital.

At the centre of the village is the Sanvitale castle, which is encircled by a moat and surrounded by ancient porticoed shops and tiled dwellings. Just outside the historic centre, 300 metres from the castle, is the site of the wartime camp. It was housed in the last of a trio of buildings on the Viale IV Novembre created by the Dominican Order of Preachers. First is the Sanctuary of the Blessed Virgin of the Sacred Rosary of Fontanellato, then the monastery of San Giuseppe, and finally the National Orphanage of the Madonna of Fontanellato.

The orphanage was paid for through donations by visitors to the Sanctuary and funds from a national appeal at the rate of 50 lire for every brick. Work began in 1928 but the building was only nearing completion in March 1943 when it was suddenly requisitioned by the Italian Government.

Instead of providing a home for little children, the orphanage became a detention centre for hundreds of Allied servicemen. It was surrounded by two fences of nine-foot high barbed wire, which were separated by a nine-foot strip of gravel. At night the area was floodlit. There were watchtowers at each corner, manned by guards with machine guns.

The camp opened on 1 April 1943. The first prisoners were transferred from the twin castles of PG 17 Rezzanello and PG 41 Montalbo in the adjoining province of Piacenza. Over the next few weeks the men were joined by contingents from camps in the south and centre of Italy: PG 21 Chieti, PG 35 Padula, PG 66 Capua, and PG 78 Sulmona.

Among the group from Montalbo was John Langrishe, a twenty-eight-year-old Cambridge law graduate and lieutenant in the Royal Artillery (RA).

He recalled:

> We were told to pack our few miserable possessions, paraded for the usual POW searches at the hands of our captors for contraband goods, and at dead of night we marched out of our mini-Colditz into a couple of large coaches, each with a passenger-carrying trailer. In these we trundled to Piacenza where a train was boarded. This took us to a station [Castelguelfo] in the middle of nowhere on a hot afternoon. Here we detrained and, weary, hot and dispirited, we had to march the couple of miles to our promised paradise...
>
> Speculation grew with every step. One voice said the camp was in huts, another that it was another castle, till finally we came in sight of a huge, new brick-built edifice. It was so impressive and modern that nobody considered for a moment that this was our destination till the head of the column turned into the gateway. We had arrived! [4]

---

[4] John Langrishe, The Long Walk Out, p 3.

The pleasurable reaction was general. Admittedly the orphanage seemed flimsy. It shook when anyone jumped up and down in one of the bedrooms. The building was also crowded and afforded little privacy. But most of the prisoners found PG 49 a nice contrast to their previous billets.

The Honourable Philip Kindersley, a captain in the Coldstream Guards, described it as 'the Ritz hotel of prison camps.'

The setting was also attractive. The building overlooks the village and plain, and on clear days there is a lovely view of the distant snow-capped Alps from upper floor windows.

The Italians arranged for the nuns next door to provide a laundry and mending service for the captives. From time to time the men found notes with their clean washing saying that the women were praying to the Madonna on their behalf. The prisoners sent back small gifts of soap, tea and chocolates with messages of thanks.

The camp was inspected on 14 May by Captain Leonardo Trippi, Attaché at the Swiss Legation in Rome, who later became an Allied helper. The neutral state had the responsibility of protecting the interests of the United Kingdom in Italy as the Protecting Power.

Swiss diplomatic representatives or delegates visited camps to monitor conditions and suggest improvements. The inspectors had access to all premises occupied by prisoners, received lists of their names, and could speak to them without witnesses. The text of the 1929 Geneva Convention relative to the Treatment of Prisoners of War had to be posted in places where it could be consulted by the captives, whenever possible in their native language.

The report, dated 24 May, noted that there were already 540 prisoners, made up of 502 soldiers, 10 sailors and 28 airmen. The camp was only 80 men short of its official capacity.

The SBO was Lieutenant Colonel DS Norman, of the East Yorkshire Regiment, known to his men as no-nonsense Norman. The majority of the detainees were British junior officers - captains, lieutenants and second lieutenants - in their twenties and thirties. There were also 114 British and South African 'other ranks.' They were detailed to act as orderlies: officers' valets or attendants, often called 'batmen.'

The Italian force guarding the prisoners consisted of Lieutenant Colonel Eugenio Vicedomini, his staff of six officers, a sergeant major, and about 60 soldiers. The colonel, a skilled bridge player, had fought alongside British troops on the border with Austria in 1917. Prior to taking command at PG 49 he had been in charge of an internment camp for Yugoslav civilians at Gonars in the Province of Udine, north-eastern Italy.

Welsh Guards captain Carol Mather related that the Italian was 'a civilised human being.' Philip Kindersley said that he was 'a very pleasant person who did everything to make our lives as bright as possible.'

Tony Davies, a Royal Artillery lieutenant, recalled:

> *The Commandant was just and equable, and gave the impression of being an excellent soldier. He was no fool and had the situation well under control. There were no loopholes. Unlike so many of his brethren, he realised that it was a POW's duty to try and escape, just as it was his duty to try and stop us. Because of his efficiency and foresight, he kept the advantage firmly with himself.* [5]

The Italian second in command at Fontanellato was even friendlier to the captives. Captain Mario Jack Camino had a British wife and mother and had been a businessman in England before the war. Described as 'more English than the English,' he was smart and charming and smoked a pipe. The captain acted as interpreter, together with his colleague Lieutenant Peredini, who had been a

---

[5] Tony Davies, When the Moon Rises, p 63.

Thomas Cook representative in Milan. However, as he was also the Security Officer, the prisoners treated him with some suspicion.

Most captives had little direct contact with Italian officers. Things were usually done through the SBO and his staff, and in any event, fraternisation was officially frowned on. Tony Davies described the rest of the officers as 'a nondescript bunch, with little to distinguish them, apart from one elderly, irritable red-faced lieutenant, popularly known as 'the Bed-bug.' As for the lowly Italian guards, most prisoners viewed them with a mixture of amusement and contempt.

In line with the Geneva Convention, both sides respected service ranks. The Italian lieutenant taking the roll call would salute the SBO. In turn, Allied junior officers saluted enemy captains and higher ranks they met officially. Eighth Hussars captain Jack Comyn - commissioned in 1935 - recalled that this practice was much resented by the wartime officers and that they did their best to avoid it. Regulars accepted the situation more willingly. In Italy rank was an obsession.

In his report, Captain Trippi said that the camp was the best his team had visited in Italy:

> *The camp covers a total area of 210,000 square feet. Ninety-two thousand square feet are covered with structures. The rest is open and can be used as sports grounds.*
>
> *The internees are quartered in a four-storied house, solidly built of stone and bricks at the beginning of the war and destined for an orphanage. The beautiful building with up-to-date installations has not yet been used for its original purpose.*
>
> *The vast premises allow the camp to be well organised. There are mess rooms for both officers and orderlies, reading rooms, a bar, a library, a high and vast hall, offices, stores for various purposes, and*

workshops. The quarters leave nothing to be desired…

The lodgings and the interior arrangements are comfortable and the camp is well organised … The morale of the internees is high. They are on excellent terms with the Commandant. The Senior Officer said in fact: 'He is perfectly agreeable.'

Offices, mess rooms and showers were located on the ground floor. The first floor was occupied by the hall, the bar, a recreation room, a barber's shop, officers' dormitories and showers. The other two floors were completely given over to accommodation and washrooms.

The officers' dormitories were high and airy. Large windows let in plenty of sun and air and overlooked the fertile plain. In every room there were two to four electric lamps and radiators for central heating. There was a dormitory holding 30 beds and other smaller ones on each floor. The SBO had a large room to himself. The officers had iron beds with elastic springs, mattresses of wool, horsehair or artificial fibre, and bed linen and two blankets. There were night tables for each bed, a wardrobe for every two officers, and tables and chairs.

The 'other ranks' had three rooms on the top floor, which were well ventilated and adequately lighted. A large dormitory accommodated 53 men and 14 corporals, and 47 others shared two interconnecting rooms. They slept in double-tier wooden beds, with a mattress and two blankets. The men also had a large corridor with tables and chairs at their disposal.

There was a small infirmary in the camp with rooms for officers and men. The medical service was superintended by an Italian surgeon. He had three officers and an attendant from among the prisoners at his command. The service was well provided with medicines and had 900 comfort and invalid parcels on hand at the time of the inspection. In an adjacent room, South African dentist, Captain Marcus Kane-Burman, had set up a busy surgery with instruments obtained from the Italians.

There was a small Roman Catholic chapel and rooms set aside for Protestant observance. They had two chaplains: a member of the Church of England and a Presbyterian.

The general part of the report concludes:

> *After our inspection round through the quarters, we sat down with the Senior [British] Officer in an office to discuss matters pertaining to the inmates of the camp - without the presence of witnesses. The officers who had some requests or claims were called in. There was no representative of the Detaining Power to listen to the conversation.*

No complaints were made to the inspectors regarding the camp. This reflects the fact that the essentials of POW life were catered for: food, shelter, clothing, and all the other items covered by the Geneva Convention.

The SBO told Captain Trippi that the kitchen was ably managed and that the food was well cooked and abundant. The catering was directed by Lieutenant Leon Blanchaert, a Belgian on the British Army's General List.

There were two kitchens on the ground floor, one for officers, and the other for the men. Both had wood-burning ranges and up-to-date equipment. The stoves were lit at five thirty in the morning, the kettles put on the range, and the fires kept burning all day. The prisoners ate in two nicely arranged messes in the basement, one for the officers and the other for the men. In their own canteens they could also purchase any foodstuffs that were not rationed.

The International Committee of the Red Cross (ICRC) in Geneva arranged for prisoners to be brought supplies of food, clothing and medicines. Parcels were prepared in the prisoners' home countries and sent in bulk to Lisbon. From there, they went to Marseilles on specially chartered Red Cross ships, and then to Geneva by train. Supplies for Italy were sent in sealed wagonloads to Milan, ready for onward transmission to the camps.

The importance of the food parcels is nicely brought out in the novel written by two lieutenants while they were held at Fontanellato. *The Cage*, by Dan Billany, from the East Yorkshire Regiment, and David Dowie, of the Royal Northumberland Fusiliers, is based on real events. They recalled that the typical five-kilogram parcel (sent to every prisoner four times a month) contained one tin each of biscuits, jam, meat and vegetables, margarine, carrots or tomatoes, meat roll, possibly bacon, cheese, and fish paste; and two tins of sugar; two ounces of tea and four of chocolate; a tin of milk; a bar of soap; raisins or porridge oats; pancake mixture; and perhaps a tinned pudding.

The officers added:

> *Without the Red Cross food we should be hungry. We have had to do it once or twice, and so we know. The rations provided by the Italians are sufficient to keep you alive for a long time, but that's about all ... When, for a short time, we had very little Red Cross food, we used to inspect the garbage tins, where sometimes we would find good cabbage stalks.* [6]

A stock of about 3,000 parcels was on hand at the time of the inspection. They were not issued to individuals as in most camps, but placed in a central store. Royal Northumberland Fusiliers captain CD (Kit) Patterson was in charge of the distribution of the food and rations. Personal items such as soap, chocolate and cigarettes were issued to the prisoners once a week. The daily food requirements were delivered to the kitchen to supplement the Italian rations.

---

[6] Dan Billany and David Dowie, The Cage, pp 6-7.

The allowance for the officers was identical to that of the civilian population, while the orderlies received the same as workmen. The daily allocation for the officers consisted of 150 grams of bread, 66 of macaroni or rice, 10 of fat, 16 of sugar, 10 of cooking cheese - and table cheese when available - 14 of meat, 15 of tomato purée, 15 of peas and beans, 7 of coffee substitute, and an egg a month. Working 'other ranks' had additional bread, cheese, macaroni or rice, but no egg.

The prisoners also had access to items from the black market. Cigarettes and other surplus items from Red Cross parcels were used to bribe guards to obtain food from farmers, including the excellent local cheese, ham and tomatoes. The float was mostly administered by ex-bank managers, to whom, Eric Newby remarked, 'this sort of thing was second nature.' The author of *Love and War in the Apennines* was a lieutenant in the Black Watch. He had been captured in August 1942 when on a special mission with the Special Boat Section in Sicily.

To pay for food and sundry expenses the captives received regular pay in camp currency. By a private arrangement between the Italian and Allied governments, the servicemen were entitled to the same remuneration as Italians of the corresponding rank.

The daily routine at PG 49 was similar to other camps. Roll call would be held in the courtyard at nine in the morning. The prisoners filed past two Italian officers to be counted. This was followed by a breakfast of tea and biscuits or porridge on Sundays. The morning was spent attending classes or playing outdoor games. After lunch, many of the men took a *siesta*. In the afternoon there was the chance for further organised activities. The second roll call would be held at six in the evening. Dinner commenced at seven.

The report says of leisure time:

A very large playground is available but it needs levelling. This will be done by the internees in order to be able to play football. The necessary material is being procured by the Commandant.

The prisoners of war can stay outdoors from eight in the morning to seven in the evening and can undertake two to three walks every week in groups of 140 officers.

There is a gallery above the large hall, furnished with tables and chairs, where the inmates of the camp can play cards and chess. A ping-pong game is also available.

A library room contains about 3,000 books. It is open for an hour in the morning and at noon when books can be taken out and exchanged. [7]

The creation of a playing field would more than double the area of the camp. Until then, the only space for exercise was a cobbled courtyard, 20 yards wide, which ran along the back of the orphanage. Work on the project allowed the one successful breakout from Fontanellato before the Armistice of September 1943.

To allow the construction work, the area was fenced off and two watchtowers added at the far end. Access was through a security gate in the middle of the courtyard. Picks and shovels were issued to the prisoners every morning after roll call and they worked till six in the evening on constructing pitches for basketball and for rugby or football. Then the implements were counted and the men filed back through the gate for evening roll call. The field would be inspected, the watchtowers closed, the guards withdrawn, and the gate locked.

The Escape Committee approved an escape attempt. A shallow trench was dug in the centre of the field that was large enough to take a man lying on his back. Gradually the space was

---

[7]   TNA: PRO WO 224/117, Report on Prisoners of War Camp no. 49.

elongated to be able to accommodate three people. They would breathe through rubber tubing. The hole was covered by planking taken from bunk beds belonging to the 'other ranks' and earth was scattered on top. The escapers' absence could be concealed for up to 48 hours. The roll call would be rigged, and two dummies made by rifle major Hugh Hope placed in beds in the dormitories for the midnight head count.

At 5.30 on the evening of Friday, 7 May, the two officers in the camp from the Welch Regiment, Captain Michael Ross and Lieutenant Jimmy Day, entered the trench. The guards were distracted by a boisterous rugby scrum. At eleven the escapers emerged, crept across the darkened field, and cut through the wire.

The officers' cover story was that they were German workers from the Fiat factory in Turin on a walking holiday. They were dressed in white shirts, air force blue trousers, and baggy jumpers concealing cloth belts. These held eight flat cocoa tins containing a daily supply of consolidated rations. The pair also carried forged identity cards and letters, currency, a hand-drawn map, compass, penknife, and razor. The bogus documents were skilfully manufactured by Royal Artillery lieutenant Michael Goldingham.[8]

The escapers decided to move at night, rest by day, and walk cross-country to minimise human contact. However, Jimmy Day fell in a weir, and his forged pass was ruined. Later the pair were forced to beg an Italian boatman to row them across the mighty River Po at Cremona, but he proved friendly and helped them on their way, quickly seeing through their disguises.

After a week, the officers started hill walking. Only 50 miles separated them from the border. They decided to press on as fast as possible, using roads, and travelling by day as well as by night.

---

[8] See my book, Special Force: SOE and the Italian Resistance 1943-1945, for Michael Goldingham's story.

Two days later the escapers were approaching Como and from the top of a ridge saw lights dotted over distant hills. As there was blackout in Italy, it could only be Switzerland.

The plan was to cross the frontier three miles north-west of the city. But a *Carabiniere* (member of the Italian army corps that is also a police force) emerged from the shadows in a side street and demanded to see their papers. The escapers ran away and the Italian blew a whistle. Two infantrymen appeared on cycles. They dismounted, unslung their rifles and ordered the runaways to halt. The freedom bid was over.

Next day the officers were returned to Fontanellato. They were ushered into the commandant's office to face a rather sad-looking colonel, who said:

> *'As yours was the first escape from this camp, I have decided not to send you to Gavi this time. From now on, occupy your minds with things other than escaping. Thirty days confinement. Dismiss.'*

Michael Ross recalled:

> *'I felt sorry for him. He was a gentleman, and our escapade had only brought him discredit.'* [9]

On Sunday, 9 May, three captains attempted another escape. The Italians were unaware that they had already lost two prisoners, and the trench lay undiscovered. Two of the newcomers were from the Royal Artillery: Tony Roncoroni, a rugby international, and Dominick Graham, known as Toby, a career soldier from the Borders. Peter Joscelyne, of the Royal Tank Regiment, had returned to Britain on the outbreak of war and risen through the ranks after a life of adventure in Argentina.

---

[9]   Michael Ross, From Liguria with Love, p 130.

The trio decided that it would be safer to only walk as far as Parma station, catch the dawn workman's train to Milan and then an express to the border town of Chiasso. Tony Roncoroni had relatives in the area who would be able to help them slip into Switzerland. The officers' cover story was that they were Spanish workers on their way from an aerodrome in Lecce to another in Como.

On the night of the escape, Toby Graham, the third man out of the trench, became entangled in a strand of the wire. His shirt was ruined and he missed the rendezvous in a vineyard a hundred yards outside the camp by 15 minutes. The officer and his two friends walked separately through the warm, moonlit night to the station.

Captains Joscelyne and Roncoroni boarded the packed Milan train at a quarter past five in the morning. They found a corner of the corridor in which to stand. No one was likely to ask awkward questions. The plain slipped by and the train made its stop at Piacenza, 57 kilometres along the line.

Policemen boarded and began to check passes. The Englishmen were confident that their documents would pass inspection. However, when it came to their turn, they were detained and marched off the train.

Captain Graham had been arrested at Parma. Then a *Carabiniere* corporal who had ushered the other two escapers on to the train suddenly remembered that they had also claimed to be Spanish workers. The police had telephoned their colleagues on Piacenza station and ordered that the officers be held on arrival.

The three captains were returned to the camp. The guards on picket duty on the night of the breakout were sentenced to two years detention. In contrast, the maximum disciplinary punishment Colonel Vicedomini could give the escapers under the Geneva Convention was 30 days confinement.

There was no punishment cell (or 'cooler') in the orphanage, just a comfortable room on the ground floor with six spring beds. Two had been optimistically labelled by the guards 'Ross' and

'Day.' As the days passed and there was still no sign of them, the captains had great fun at the expense of Captain Camino. But on the evening of the tenth day, Michael Ross and Jimmy Day were pushed into the room.

The Italians thought that the escapers had left at the same time. The playing field was placed out of bounds while the guards tried to discover the means of escape. Eventually one of the search party stumbled into the trench. To jeers and cheers from the orphanage, a morning was spent trying to recreate the escape. The Italians attempted to pack five small men into the hollow. Finally they admitted defeat. The troops returned to the guardroom covered in mud.

Later in the war, Michael Ross escaped to Monte Carlo. At the end of 1946 he married Giovanna Porcheddu, twin daughter of one of the Italian families that had sheltered him. Jimmy Day successfully crossed Allied lines in the south. So too did Toby Graham and Tony Roncoroni.

In contrast, in August 1943 Peter Joscelyne was ordered to appear before an angry general at PG 49 to account for a letter he had written from the camp at Chieti that was critical of the Italians.

The captain refused to apologise or to back down and was sent to the high security PG 5 Gavi in Piedmont, whose inmates had made at least one escape attempt from another camp. The prisoners were deported to Germany on the Armistice the following month.

3

Hopes of Freedom

While the camp at Fontanellato was convulsed by a dramatic escape attempt, events over a thousand miles away in North Africa ensured the future course of the war in Italy.

On 13 May 1943 almost a quarter of a million Germans and Italians surrendered to Montgomery's Eighth Army in Tunisia. At the Casablanca Conference in January, Winston Churchill and United States president Franklin D Roosevelt had agreed that Sicily would be invaded after the defeat of the last Axis forces in North Africa. Now the project to take the Italian island as the prelude to the invasion of the mainland entered its operative phase. The mission was given the codename of Husky.

The changing tide of war seemed to offer the prospect of early release for the 80,000 Allied prisoners of war held in Italy. But they remained isolated behind bars. At Fontanellato the men's only window on the outside world was in the escorted walks they were allowed to make in the area around the camp. On average, the opportunity came round for an individual about once every 10 days, not two or three times a week as suggested in the inspector's report. The excursions took place before breakfast. The captives were on parole, having given their word not to try to escape. But they were still heavily guarded. The men would deliberately march at the double along quiet country lanes, leaving the reservist guards huffing and puffing in pursuit.

For most of the day, the captives' time was their own. Lectures were given on a wide variety of subjects, including agriculture, law, languages, and journalism. Textbooks were obtained from other camps, the British Legation in the Vatican, the Red Cross, or from families at home. The binding of hardbacks was always torn off by the Italian censors in search of concealed maps, but they were repaired by the prisoners using card from Red Cross parcels.

Sports and entertainments were run by RAF Flying Officer Bill Rainford. He had been captured in Libya on 10 June 1940, the day Italy entered the war. Football was especially popular despite the heat. The surface of the pitch became rock hard. Games were played for 15 minutes each way in the mornings and evenings. There were 22 teams in a seven-a-side league, with a cup as the prize. Rugby was also played and the South African 'other ranks' team beat all comers.

Athletic contests and boxing matches were organised and even a race for boats made from wine corks. They bobbed along a little stream that ran between the courtyard and the playing field. One of the prisoners recalled: 'I at once came to the conclusion that all the officers taking part in this sport were completely round the bend. However, within a fortnight I was one of the most enthusiastic of boat owners!'

Two bookmaking firms emerged to cater for the large betting fraternity. The odds were advertised on the notice board in the hall. Football pools were the most popular. Flying Officer Rainford even managed to persuade Lieutenant Peredini to have betting slips printed by a firm in Parma.

Bill Rainford also ran a popular organisation called 'Opportunities Limited,' or 'Ops.' It covered almost every aspect of camp life apart from organising a means of escape. In one of his earlier camps, the officer had noticed the volume of items that the prisoners swapped in an uncoordinated and haphazard way. He decided to set up a liaison service.

The enterprise operated from rooms between 10 to 12 in the morning, and in the bar at opening times. It offered an attractive range of goods and services and advertised on the notice board with the slogan 'Whatever you want we'll try to find. Whatever you don't want we'll sell. Sole and maximum charge five per cent to seller. No job too large or too small.' The venture was a great success and to avoid racketeering was officially designated the only means of sale and exchange.

English tobacco and cigarettes were always in stock. Pipes were repaired, and also deck chairs. Tankards were made, raffles run and letters written. An art department painted portraits, landscapes and miniatures, framed pictures, and designed cards and social stationery. Books were bound and watches repaired. Badges, wings, or pips were embroidered, collars fitted on shirts, and socks darned. On one memorable occasion, the team even retrieved a Dunhill cigarette lighter that had disappeared down a bend in the toilet.

Many prisoners played bridge and backgammon in the assembly hall, or baccarat after dinner in the mess. It was possible to hire a piano and to buy musical instruments, and several groups were formed to provide music for concerts and stage shows. There was a dramatics group, and an artist's circle that organised a memorable exhibition of landscape and portrait paintings.

Tickets were issued to the officers for the purchase of a glass of wine and Vermouth per day. A bar was opened in a section of the gallery above the assembly hall. It was run at lunchtime and in the evenings by 11th Hussars lieutenant Tommy Pitman and his team. If a party were going to be held, the host would buy tickets from other prisoners with cigarettes or chocolate. As a result, Eric Newby recalled, 'there were some good parties and some rather awful ones too.'

The captives were forbidden from standing at the windows of the bar. Those who disobeyed the order risked being shot at by the sentries in the watchtowers. However, the lure of seeing passing village girls and evacuees from Parma in their silk stockings proved too strong for the men. As a result, the stained glass windows of the bar had been shot away long ago and the walls and ceiling were peppered with bullet holes, like in some Wild West saloon.

Stuart Hood, the left-wing writer and broadcaster, a lieutenant in the Highland Light Infantry, wrote later that the prisoners at PG 49 fell roughly into three categories:

> *Those whose lives were adjusted to an orderly and not unpleasant routine, such as they had known before in prep or public school. Those who played at escaping - carting spoil from impossible tunnels, conspiring endlessly and fruitlessly. Those who rebelled, who dismissed camp activities - games, discussions, study groups - as opiates; whose motto was the old revolutionary one 'the worse the better;' who had the revolutionary's patience, lack of scruple and love of mystery. A few were outside any category. They were the ones who had to be watched in case, in broad daylight, they simply got up and jumped the wire. It was difficult to know what they desired more: to escape or to be killed.* [10]

Carol Mather thought that there were two main types of prisoners: traditional escapers and 'a more intellectual group who had become accustomed to a monastic life of books, learning and artistic endeavour.' They were 'the lotus-eating school,' who believed that 'escapees were simply on an ego trip and ruined the life of everyone else who were inevitably penalised.'

Class was ever present at Fontanellato, as in all British officer camps. Eric Newby wrote that PG 49 'was more like a public school' than any other prison camp he knew:

> *It was the upper class which set the style in the orfanotrofio [orphanage], just as they had done in the pre-war world outside ... These amateur soldiers, for they were mostly amateurs, and any professional*

---

[10] Stuart Hood, Carlino, p 9.

soldiers who had the same sort of background
(any others were soon made into figures of fun), made
up the coteries of OK people who exercised power.

The elite were very reluctant to consort with outsiders at all, explained Newby, but had to in the larger dormitories. They always tried to ensure that the beds were occupied by those they considered marginally acceptable:

The sort of people they were prepared to talk to and
drink with while the war was on, and then would never
see again. And this included a number of people whom
they regarded as being downright common but who had
the saving grace of being funny...
Everyone else they ignored completely, unless they
owned something worth buying, or had some skill which
they could make use of to increase their comfort. It was
not that they consigned these unfortunates to outer
darkness; they simply never invited them in out of it.[11]

After the failure of the May breakout, more conventional methods of escape were tried, though tunnelling was difficult as the camp was based upon a single building. Any shaft would have to start in the basement, which was searched every day.

A tunnel launched by the Guards was discovered within a week. As a result, the Italians dug a ten-foot deep trench around the camp, just above the level of the water table. This wiped out tunnelling as a means of escape.

Still, a major project was launched at the end of June. It was designed to create a hiding place within the orphanage. Italy's days in the war seemed numbered. There was the fear that prisoners would be transported to Germany, quickly, efficiently

---

[11] Eric Newby, Love and War in the Apennines, p 38.

and without warning. A small number of prisoners could scuttle to the hide if the Germans took over, and stay there till the building was empty. The project was masterminded by Royal Artillery captain Michael Gilbert, the solicitor and writer, who completed his POW murder mystery, *Death in Captivity*, in the camp. His helpers in the excavation included Tony Davies, Toby Graham, and Eric Newby, who in his memoir described digging a tunnel as 'the most dreary and unimaginative way of getting out of any prison.'

Using an improvised hammer and chisel, the team lifted nine tiles in the corner of a ground floor room, mounted them on a wooden frame to make a trap door, and dug into the concrete floor. After a month the men struck diagonally through the outside wall. The aim was to burrow into a cavity under the main steps of the building. But the work never got that far as it was overtaken by events.

Lieutenant Colonel Robert Williams, from the 4th Gurkha Rifles, told me that in 1982 he and his wife visited the former camp. It was empty and the caretaker showed them around. When they came to the loft, much of the floor between the joists was covered by earth and stones, which the Italian said was the spoil from escape attempts.

Over the summer of 1943, even the traditional escapers came to believe that the changing tide of war might ensure their early release. The privacy of the prison world was dissolving.

Dan Billany wrote:

> *Our sense of isolation as a community was progressively destroyed at Fontanellato by the news of the progress of the war. The offensive in North Africa began again, and in May Tunis and Bizerta fell. North Africa, where we had nearly all been captured in what seemed an endless scuffle, was now entirely British. Barce, Derna, Benghazi, all these Axis bases where we had*

languished as prisoners were now full of British troops. The power of Britain had stepped decisively towards us and freedom became a thing to bear in mind.[12]

News of the fighting was also provided by a trickle of new arrivals. Many came not from the 8th but from the 1st Army, which served in Algiers and Tunisia.

There were now about ten lieutenant colonels in the camp. Among them was Hugh Mainwaring of the Royal Artillery, whose family home was at Llanfyllin in Montgomeryshire. He had been the senior general staff officer in charge of Operations (GSO 1) at General Montgomery's HQ. After the battle of El Alamein the colonel had moved forward to find a new site for the headquarters, but had been captured by German rearguard troops near Mersa Matruh.

The officer gave four popular lectures on the desert war from 1940-1942. He provided the men with a broad view of the battles, and insights into the general's likely future strategy and tactics, which proved uncannily correct.

Fresh from the defeat of all Axis forces in North Africa, the Allies invaded Sicily on 10 July in Operation Husky. On the night of 24th-25th July, Mussolini was overthrown in a palace coup and speedily replaced by Marshal Pietro Badoglio.

The news arrived at Fontanellato in a radio news broadcast, which was relayed over a loudspeaker above the Italian Orderly Room at eight in the morning on the 25th.

The guards poured out of their huts, dancing with joy, and

---

[12] Dan Billany and David Dowie, The Cage, pp 143-4. A note in the front of the book records that the authors' 'fates are unknown.' They are believed to have disappeared in the Apennines. The manuscript was left with the Meletti farming family at Soragna, five miles from PG 49, who sent it to Dan Billany's parents in the spring of 1946.

tore down portraits of the dictator from the walls and trod them underfoot. The Italians thought it meant the end of the war for them.

The Fascist salute was abandoned, posters destroyed and busts of Mussolini smashed. Prisoners walking under guard in the countryside next day were amused to see that the Fascist emblems on kilometre posts, house number plaques and public buildings had already been removed or painted over. On walls and the side of houses, the slogan, 'Long Live the King' had replaced 'Mussolini is always right.'

Larry Allen, an American war correspondent from the Associated Press, placed regular news bulletins on the notice board. They were skilfully blended to hide the fact that as well as being drawn from items in the Italian newspapers, they relied upon Allied broadcasts received over an illicit radio. Its precise location in the camp was a carefully guarded secret. The set had been made from tins obtained from Red Cross parcels, camp wire and valves that had been brought in by devious means from outside.

Every news report began with the word 'Flash.' The one on Mussolini's fall read in suitably large letters: 'Flash, *Benito finito!*'

It was universally thought in Italy that after a short interval the war would end. The prisoners began to lay bets on the date when they would be able to walk out of the camp gates as free men.

4

The 45 Days

At eleven on the evening of Sunday, 25 July 1943, Marshal Pietro Badoglio, non-Fascist successor to the deposed Mussolini, made his first radio broadcast to the nation and dashed hopes of an early peace:

> *Italians! On the orders of His Majesty the King Emperor, I have today assumed the military government of the country with full powers. The war continues alongside our German ally ... The command I have received is clear and precise and it will be carried out scrupulously.*
>
> *Anyone who harbours illusions of being able to obstruct lawful change, or who tries to disturb public order will be punished severely.*
>
> *Long live Italy! Long live the King!*

For the 45 days of its existence (25 July to 8 September) the government was forced to maintain a precarious balancing act between the competing demands of conservatives and anti-fascist parties at home and the Germans and the Allies abroad.

The Fascist Party was dissolved and political prisoners were released, but assemblies and meetings were banned. Marshal Badoglio promised that political life would be resumed at the end of the war. For the moment, the Italians were asked only to have faith in the government.

The King and the Marshal desperately wanted peace, but had to make a pretence of continuing the war in an attempt to avoid the risk of the Germans seizing power. In the meantime, extra German divisions poured over the Brenner Pass, Allied bombing raids continued and strikes and food riots broke out in the cities.

Detailed plans for a probable Italian capitulation were agreed between the British and United States governments on 3 August. As decided at Casablanca in January, the only terms on offer were unconditional surrender. On the same day, an Italian diplomat made peace overtures to the British ambassador in Lisbon. Secret negotiations continued throughout the month. They took place in Tangiers and Madrid, and in Rome itself with the assistance of an SOE wireless operator, Lieutenant Richard Mallaby.

Churchill insisted on: 'The immediate liberation of all British prisoners of war in Italian hands, and the prevention, which can in the first instance only be by the Italians, of their being transported northwards to Germany.' The new Italian Foreign Minister, Raffaele Guariglia, turned down a German request to hand the men over.

Ever since Axis forces surrendered to the Allies in North Africa in May it had been clear to everyone that the invasion of Italy was likely. Camps in the Naples area and in the rest of the south were closed. Most of the inmates were moved to prisons elsewhere in Italy, but two thousand were transferred to Germany. By September 1943 the camps in the south had all been abandoned, though a few prisoners remained in hospitals, gaols, or isolated work detachments. Prison camps in the regions of Lazio and the Abruzzo were now closest to the front line.

A few categories of captives were eligible for early release and repatriation. A mixed medical commission in the camps considered claims from prisoners based upon serious illness, age or infirmity. Surplus medical personnel were also eligible, and there were sometimes requests from captured war correspondents on the grounds that they were non-combatants. Otherwise, only the changing tide of war or local initiatives would ensure the ending of the indeterminate term as a prisoner of war.

The month of August was a peaceful one at Fontanellato. Once hopes of early release began to fade, an intense feeling of anti-climax enveloped the camp. The only cloak and dagger activity was the preparation of maps and the forging of identity cards.

One unexpected change was that the mail speeded up. Prisoners of war were allowed to send and receive correspondence, packages, money orders and telegrams. Now letters and parcels from the United Kingdom took only 10 days to arrive instead of an average 65 days earlier in the year. Censorship of the contents seemed to have largely been abandoned.

The guards no longer fired at the windows of the bar when the prisoners looked out of them. But the walks were cancelled. The authorities seemed to fear that a friendlier populace might pose security risks.

Lieutenant Jack Comyn made one of the last attempts to escape from PG 49. He took advantage of the fact that twice a week he was required to help an Italian Quartermaster Sergeant (QMS) in a clothing store just outside the wire. The building housed garments confiscated by the Italians from prisoners' parcels, fearing that they might be used for escape purposes. The lieutenant dealt with the paperwork required to issue receipts in English. He managed to have his friend Major Hugh Hope appointed as his assistant. The major had created the two dummies used in the earlier breakout, as we saw in chapter two.

Early one afternoon, Hugh Hope distracted the Italian QMS in one room while Jack Comyn did a quick change in the other. He donned some of the clothing and a workman's hat, rubbed himself with dust from the floor, picked up a hammer, and jumped through the window.

Jack Comyn recalled:

I looked around. There seemed to be nobody about. I had to walk along this road, past the front of the camp, with its wire fence and sentry towers, to get clear. All went well until the road veered away towards the village. Suddenly a man in uniform stepped from behind a tree in front of me. I knew him well, he was the Brigadiere (a rank roughly equivalent to sergeant) of the Carabiniere detachment which supplemented the camp guards. 'Dove andate?' [Where are you going?] he addressed me. Alas, my Italian was not good enough to maintain any pretence of being a building worker, certainly in face of a member of the Carabinieri Reali, one of the best police forces in Europe.

Within a few minutes I was ushered into the office of the Camp Commandant. This was Colonnello Vicedomini, an elderly officer recalled from retirement. He was of the old school, a perfect gentleman, liked by all. The Brigadiere told him that I was Tenente [Lieutenant] Comyn, caught while trying to escape. I was still in my disguise, and at first the Colonel refused to believe that it was me. When convinced, his consternation was amazing.

'But, Tenente Comyn,' he exclaimed, 'my sentries on the wire might have shot you - and then what would your mother have said?'

As I had not expected this question I was uncertain how to reply, but his concern touched me, and I received with equanimity the statutory sentence of 28 days solitary confinement which he awarded.

The sentence was served in the large room on the ground floor that functioned as a punishment cell. Jack Comyn was allowed out for exercise once a day, had his meals brought to him, and had plenty of books and magazines to read. With the connivance of some of the guards, he also received visits from friends, who brought little treats. Jack Comyn recalled: 'I do not think I spent a more delightful four weeks in the whole of my captivity.'[13]

In early August a new SBO arrived from PG 202 Lucca Prisoner of War Hospital: Lieutenant Colonel Hugo Graham de Burgh, of the Royal Artillery, a member of an upper class Anglo-Irish family. Aged 49, the officer had a record of distinguished service in the First World War, during which he was wounded twice. He served in India and Africa and was captured during Rommel's 1942 offensive.

The colonel was Senior British Officer at three prison camps before coming to Fontanellato. While in the hospital at Lucca, he had heard rumours of Allied prisoners of war being sent to Germany, which, as we have already seen, turned out to be true.

Colonel de Burgh found the captives at PG 49 demoralised. He asserted command and arranged for them to learn new skills and to prepare themselves physically for escape. Meanwhile, to meet any emergency, a company structure was superimposed upon the dormitory organisation.

Eric Newby recalled the changes:

> *Although the senior officer thought he ran the camp it was really run by people elected by the coteries, just like Pop [the elite society] at Eton, where so many of them had been.*
>
> *This state of affairs continued until a very regular full colonel arrived who had not been at Eton but at Wellington and was so horrified by the lackadaisical, demilitarised state in which he found us all that he immediately organised the camp on the lines of an infantry battalion, in companies with company*

---

[13] Jack Comyn, Episodes, p 84.

> *commanders. Under him the orfanotrofio began to*
> *resemble the prison camp in Renoir's Grande Illusion.*
> *It had a commandant who was a regular colonnello of*
> *the ancien régime who found himself in sympathy with*
> *our colonel, who came from the same sort of background*
> *as he did.*[14]

Five companies were created, four for officers and one for the 'other ranks.' Each unit was composed of around a hundred men, with its own commander (who was a lieutenant colonel), an adjutant, platoons, sections, and an infantry component. There were drills and duty rosters and the men were ordered to tidy up their appearance. The changes also meant that roll call could be carried out in a much more orderly manner. The SBO made an Italian speaker his ADC: the outspoken Stuart Hood. Lieutenant Colonel Hugh Mainwaring became Chief of Staff and another gunner lieutenant colonel, Richard Wheeler, was appointed Intelligence Officer.

On 17 August the Italians announced that Sicily had been captured, only 38 days after it was invaded. They seemed completely calm and resigned to the idea that the war had been lost.

Relations with the prisoners improved. Toby Graham commented: 'The Germans would probably have become more difficult to deal with as things got worse for them; not so the wily Latin who steadily became more pleasant.'

A seven-course celebration dinner with a Sicilian theme was held in the mess and a new wave of optimism swept the camp. Everyone waited for news of the mainland invasion.

Tony Davies related that the consensus was 'that the Germans would make no attempt to hold southern and central Italy, but would rapidly withdraw to the line of the Po, or even to the Austrian frontier.' He added that logically the idea might seem ridiculous.

---

[14] Eric Newby, Love and War in the Apennines, p 44.

Even apart from the German reaction to what they were bound to consider an act of treachery on the part of their ally, Italy presented the most perfect defensive country in Europe:

> *However, prisoners are not logical people, and the thought that the Nazis would do anything but make a very rapid - albeit fighting - withdrawal never entered our minds. What did enter our minds, however, was the probability that in the course of this retreat the Boche would grab all the prisoners he could. The fact that our camp was so far north did not make us any happier, and the tension mounted almost to breaking point during the last days of August.* [15]

In the week after the fall of Sicily was announced a mighty drone of aircraft was heard overhead. The prisoners cheered as a formation of United States planes swept across the camp in a south-westerly direction, the sun glinting on their fuselages. It was learned later that the aircraft had flown from bases in Britain to bomb the ball-bearing factory at Regensburg in Germany and were making for Algiers.

The planes were quickly identified as the Boeing B-17 Flying Fortress, a four-engined heavy bomber. However, an aircraft at the tail of the group was seen to be losing height and smoke began to pour from its engines. A parachute was seen to drift down and a few moments later the bomber disappeared behind trees and exploded. There would be no other survivors from the seven-man crew.

Soldiers were sent in the camp truck to detain the American. An hour later he was brought into the Italian offices just outside

---

[15] Tony Davies, When the Moon Rises, pp 78-9. The lieutenant was recaptured when nearing the Sangro. One of his companions, Hal Becker, was shot during the attempt to cross the lines, but two others, Michael Gilbert and Toby Graham, were successful.

the wire. The airman was on crutches and helped by two of the guards. He was soon driven away, but not before the prisoners had sent him a Red Cross parcel, the quickest delivery ever recorded.

John Langrishe related that in August:

> *Pictures appeared in the papers of 'the armoured train,' a pathetic collection of antique railway ironmongery, featuring a large but almost prehistoric cannon, which was being sent to the toe of Italy to guard the coast against landings. It could not have lasted more than a few hours from the attentions of the RAF, if indeed it ever reached a war zone.*
>
> *Another strange thing happened. One day, out of the blue, that much respected newspaper the Corriere della Sera appeared with the front page and also much of the second covered with a most fulsome praise for l'Ottava Armata, the British 8th Army, describing its victories and defeats but holding it up as an example of perfect military conduct and behaviour.*
>
> *This was clearly a step in preparing the Italian people for a change of side in the war. When it actually arrived, the people could rely on the British Army to regard them as friends again. Only shortly before, the papers had been reviling the 'barbarous Anglo-Saxon fliers' who had been dropping bombs on their sacred soil.*
>
> *Further sensations came hot on the heels of one another. Now the Allies were ashore on the mainland near Reggio di Calabria. Behind our barbed wire, we began to envisage freedom within a matter of days...*
>
> *One small worry, however, clouded our otherwise encouraging outlook: how would the German Army react?* [16]

---

[16] John Langrishe, The Long Walk Out, p 7.

Jack Comyn recalled that they had already seen German troops:

A large unit marched past our camp, singing loudly as only German soldiers can, clearly out to intimidate us. We yelled back, and one could almost feel the hackles rising on both sides of the wire. I was impressed by the bearing of these soldiers and by their horse transport, all the leather of saddles and traces clearly brand new.[17]

On 3 September, The Instrument of Armistice and Surrender of the Italian Forces to the Commander-in-Chief of the Allied Forces, General Dwight D Eisenhower, was signed in an olive grove at Cassibile, near Syracuse, in Sicily. Before dawn, the British Eighth Army had crossed the Straits of Messina to enter the mainland.

The military terms were set out in 12 brief conditions. For our story, the most interesting is the third:

All prisoners or internees of the United Nations are to be immediately turned over to the Allied Commander-in-Chief, and none of these may now or at any time be evacuated to Germany.

The surrender was secret. The conditions of the Armistice could not be made public without the prior approval of General Eisenhower. For five more days the Italian nation would remain in limbo.

The Italian War Office sent an order to its Camp Commandants on 6 September:

British POWs - Prevent them falling into German hands. In the event that it is not possible to defend efficiently

---

[17] Jack Comyn, op. cit., p 87.

*all the camps, set at liberty all the white prisoners but
keep the blacks in prison.*

*Facilitate their escape either to Switzerland or along
the Adriatic coast to southern Italy. Labour units in
civilian clothes may also be helped, provided they are
away from the German line of retreat. At the opportune
moment the freed prisoners should be given reserve rations
and directions as to which route they should follow.*

Colonel de Burgh recalled a conversation with Colonel
Vicedomini at this point:

*He informed me that the Germans had intimated that
prisoners were to be removed to Germany. I asked him
what he intended to do and if he was prepared to give
us some warning. He replied that he would, and that if
I organised inside the wire, he would have cyclists out to
bring information of any approach of German troops.*

Two days later, on Wednesday, 8 September, celebrations were
going on in the village of Fontanellato. It was second traditional
festival of the year to honour the Madonna, the *Sagra* at the
approach of autumn.

At 7.43 in the evening, transmissions on Italian radio were
suddenly interrupted. A sad song called *A Road in the Wood* had
been playing, but a recorded message by Marshal Badoglio came
on air instead:

*The Italian Government, recognising the impossibility of
continuing the unequal struggle against vastly superior
forces, and with the intention of avoiding even more severe
damage to the nation, has asked General Eisenhower,
Commander-in-Chief of the Anglo-American allied
forces, for an armistice.*

*The request has been accepted. Consequentl_
hostile act towards the Anglo-American forces on th_
of Italian forces must cease everywhere. However, _
will respond to possible attacks from any other quarter.*

John Langrishe recalled the arrival of the news at the camp:

*I had come back to my room after supper and was
chatting with two or three others when the serenity
of the summer evening was shattered by a growing
hubbub from the direction of the village. We went to the
windows and soon were astonished to see a large crowd
of villagers, joined by our guards, come hurrying down
the road, some on bicycles and some on foot, shouting,
singing, cheering, and throwing their caps in the air.
'Peace, peace,' they cried, suiting the action to the words.
The soldiers flung down their rifles, jumped on them,
and called out to us that we were now their friends.*

*Our first reaction was perhaps one of numbness.
Here was the thing we had all been waiting for, and
what were we to do? Were we free to leave the camp?
Would our troops be with us in the morning? How
would we be sent home? These and a hundred other
like questions sprang into our minds, until through the
chatter of excited conversation came the order that the
Senior British Officer would address all ranks in the
main hall immediately.*[18]

Colonel de Burgh said:

*Gentlemen, I have been informed by the Commandant
that the Italian Government has asked for an armistice.*

---

[18] John Langrishe, op. cit., p 8.

Beyond that I know nothing, but he has promised to keep me in immediate touch with the situation. In the meantime, it is absolutely essential that everyone keeps perfectly calm and behaves like a British officer. No one is to look out of the windows or make demonstrations of any kind with the civilians. No one is allowed outside the building.

Everyone will parade in the courtyard at nine tomorrow morning, when I will give you further details of the situation. [19]

At the time, there were 536 prisoners of war at Fontanellato, made up of 483 officers and 53 men. Four hundred and twenty-eight of the captives were British Army personnel, 39 South African Army, 27 Indian Army, 2 New Zealand Army, 1 Canadian Army, 20 Royal Air Force, 17 Royal Navy. There were also two war correspondents, the Briton Ronnie Noble and Larry Allen from the United States.

The prisoners went to bed in a state of nervous excitement. Lookouts were posted in top floor rooms. What would the morning bring?

---

[19] The Hon. Philip Kindersley, For You the War is Over, p 70.

5

The Mass Escape

The prisoners of war in Fontanellato camp rose early on Thursday, 9 September 1943, after receiving news the night before of the Armistice. Everyone was on parade at five to nine to hear the orders of the Senior British Officer, Lieutenant Colonel Hugo de Burgh. It was the first time that there were no Italians present.

The colonel stated that some time ago he had received an order from the War Office through the usual channels. It instructed that in the event of an armistice everyone in prison camps should stay put. The SBO said that he believed that the order was out of date and did not reflect the true tactical situation.

Colonel Vicedomini had received information that there had been fighting since dawn in Parma and Piacenza between German and Italian troops. It was likely that the Germans would arrive at any moment to take over the camp. If this happened, the Commandant had said that he would defend the village with the force under his command.

Colonel de Burgh stated that he had considered offering the services of his men to help the Italians, but had decided that he did not wish to do anything that might embarrass the British Government.

A place was being found in the countryside where all the prisoners could be hidden. The Commandant had scouts on the access roads to give early warning of any move on the camp.

The alarm signal would be three Gs blown on a bugle. If it

were sounded, the men would quickly assemble in companies and march out through a large gap cut in the wire by the Italians at the top end of the playing field.

Once the parade was over, the prisoners were to don battledress, collect a day's rations, and be ready to evacuate the camp at five minutes notice. They were also to familiarise themselves with their emergency stations.

The Commandant issued the prisoners with small amounts of Lire. The men tidied their rooms and packed away items that they might be able to recover later. They exchanged addresses and passed on messages for their families in case of trouble on the way.

The work done, the captives chatted in the courtyard over a mid-morning drink of cocoa. Suddenly two JU88 German bombers swooped low over the camp. The men scattered and dived to the ground, but the planes disappeared without taking any hostile action.

The prisoners' information service was in overdrive. Allied landings were reported at Genoa, La Spezia, Leghorn, and Trieste. Rumours from the camp staff were even more encouraging. It seemed that the situation would soon be under control and that the Germans would be forced to quit Italy.

Philip Kindersley wrote: 'Had we not had this completely erroneous information, the majority of us would have adopted very different tactics during the next few days, and many more of us would have succeeded in reaching our own lines.' He described his time later in the Bardi area as 'seven wasted weeks' before beginning the great trek south.[20]

The bar was even busier than normal. In the kitchens, Lieutenant Blanchaert and his team began to prepare a special lunch of cold salmon and new potatoes.

---

[20] Philip Kindersley was recaptured together with Scots Guards captain Ronald Orr-Ewing near Gubbio on 3 December 1943 after walking 400 miles.

One British officer was already outside the wire. Lieutenant Colonel Hugh Mainwaring had been given responsibility for coordinating the response to any emergency. Once news arrived of the invasion, he had been tasked with finding a refuge for the prisoners if the rapid evacuation of the camp became necessary.

The Commandant had called on Hugh Mainwaring at 7.30 in the morning and said that the situation had deteriorated. He gave him a map of the area and suggested the best direction to take. Accompanied by Captain Camino, the officer left the camp half an hour later. They found a suitable hiding place five miles north-west of the camp. The deep, winding bed of the Rovacchia torrent has steep banks covered with scrub, beeches and poplars.

As the pair arrived back at the camp at noon, a patrol returned with the news that a German column had been sighted only two miles away. It was drawn up on the main road and was ready to take over the camp.

Colonel Vicedomini was true to his word. An Italian bugler blew three Gs, the prearranged alarm signal. Stuart Hood recalled the sound of feet running in the corridors of the orphanage, shouts, laughter, and commands as the prisoners sprinted down to the courtyard.

For the last time the men paraded in their five companies. They marched out through the gap in the wire, led by Colonel Mainwaring and Captain Camino. The escapers walked three in a row, creating a long, straggling column. It was hoped that the crew of any German aircraft would judge the formation to be one of their own infantry battalions.

Some of the Italian soldiers who had helped plan the departure joined their captain in the column, including Lieutenant Peredini and Sergeant Major Rissotto. Colonel Vicedomini and 40 of his troops chose to remain.

The march out was done quietly and in good order. By 12.10 the camp was empty.

The walk to the hiding place took two hours. The country lanes were sweltering in the afternoon sun, but no one seemed to mind, they were so happy. Toby Graham recalled: 'One moment we were prisoners behind wire - the next, free men walking through sunlit vineyards, plucking at the near-ripe grapes.'

The only incident was the appearance of a solitary German Junkers 52 aircraft. It swooped so low over the column that the airmen could hardly have failed to notice the prisoners' khaki battledress and the large red prisoner of war diamond sown on the back.

The escapers spread out along the watercourse according to the areas assigned to each company by Hugh Mainwaring. They were ordered to stay together and take cover in the surrounding trees, vineyards and fields of Indian corn. If rescue were at hand, the escapers could return to the camp. If not, they were in a good position to disperse.

A few officers thought that this approach was tantamount to waiting to be rounded up by the Germans, and decided to leave immediately. They included Carol Mather, who slipped away together with rifle captain Archie Hubbard. The pair crossed British forward positions near Campobasso, the capital of the Molise region, in mid-October.

In spite of the precautions taken to disguise the escapers' presence by the stream, a steady trickle of Italians began to come across the fields. They brought supplies from Red Cross parcels and news of what had happened at the camp.

Two hours after the prisoners had fled, two German armoured cars and about 30 infantrymen in lorries arrived. They fired shots over the heads of villagers who were carrying off supplies from the camp and stores. Two days later, the Germans announced that looting would be treated as a capital offence, but for the orphanage it was too late. Everything moveable had gone.

Local historian Marco Minardi has provided an eyewitness account of the arrival of the Germans in the testimony of a soldier who was a native of Fontanellato. Dario Fava, of the Third Bersaglieri Regiment, had arrived at the camp in the morning, carrying orders from Milan for Colonel Vicedomini, who was also an infantryman.

The soldier recalled that the Commandant received the instruction to liberate the prisoners at around 10.30 or 10.45:

> *On their arrival, the Germans glimpsed the colonel. An SS lieutenant, accompanied by Pietralunga the interpreter, approached him and said: 'Where are the prisoners?'*
>
> *'I had the order to liberate them,' replied Vicedomini. He barely had time to say this when the German lieutenant struck him savagely. Then he took away the pistol in the colonel's bandoleer and ordered his men to disarm all the soldiers. The Germans made us go to the command centre and stash our weapons there.*[21]

The Germans dined on the cold salmon and new potatoes prepared for the prisoners, drank a lot of wine, and vandalised as much of the camp as they could. Finally, after loading their trucks with booty, the soldiers drove off. Then the villagers returned.

Colonel Vicedomini was taken away by the Germans, together with his remaining officers, and sent to a POW camp in Poland. At the end of the war he returned to Italy in broken health and died soon afterwards. Colonel de Burgh described the colonel as 'extremely kind and helpful during our meetings,' adding, 'he organised our escape and our shelter.'

In the evening the companies were ordered to consolidate their positions around the stream. The men spent a warm night under the stars. The roar of motorised transport could be heard from the main road and mysterious flashes lit the distant horizon.

---

[21] Marco Minardi, L'Orizzonte del Campo, pp 45-6.

Shortly after dawn a procession of farmers and villagers began arriving in the encampment with clothing, money and food supplies for the escapers. Other donations were solicited by Captain Camino and Lieutenant Peredini and by local anti-Fascists. By the evening, 200 officers and men had also been found billets on farms. All the Italians in the district knew where the prisoners were, but no one betrayed them to the Germans. The civilians also brought unbelievable news of Allied advances, supposedly heard on the radio.

Over the following days, girls on bicycles ferried food and clothing to the men in hiding, travelling only in pairs so as not to attract suspicion from any Germans or Fascists they met. One of the cyclists was Wanda Skof, Eric Newby's future wife.

During that Friday, Colonel de Burgh called a conference.

Jack Comyn recalled:

> *Colonel de Burgh and Hugh Mainwaring had anxious consultations, in which I took part because Hugh had enlisted me as a kind of staff officer, together with Captain Blanchaert ... The SBO considered that he had obeyed the War Office orders, in that he had so far kept us all together. But it was clearly impossible to continue feeding 500 of us in the ravine, and the Germans might at any moment discover where we were.*

Colonel de Burgh announced that in view of the danger from German troops in the area, the companies would leave the Rovacchia. They would move west and then stand down. The men would be free to attempt to cross the Swiss border, or to join friendly forces in the south, though they were over 600 miles away. The dispersal would take place over the next two days. Philip Kindersley wrote of the SBO: 'His decision proved one hundred per cent correct, and those officers who were lucky enough to get home have Colonel de Burgh to thank for their good fortune.'

Captain Camino guided the colonel and his two staff officers, Lieutenant Colonel Richard Wheeler and Captain Reggie Phillips, to his home region of the Val d'Aosta. As it was thought that a party of three would be too conspicuous, Colonel Wheeler went off on his own.

After four days of hard and dangerous climbing, Colonel de Burgh and Captain Phillips took smugglers' trails to reach Zermatt in Switzerland on 29 September. Soon they heard that Colonel Wheeler had also been successful. So too were the enterprising flying officer Bill Rainford and the earlier SBO from Fontanellato, Lieutenant Colonel DS Norman, who had been held at PG 29 Veano on the Armistice.

In October 1945 Colonel de Burgh became head of the Allied Screening Commission, which had been set up to recognise and compensate persons who had assisted Allied personnel behind enemy lines after the 1943 armistice.

Colonel Hugh Mainwaring was one of the earliest to leave the encampment. Lieutenant Comyn, who had been acting as one of his assistants, was asked to join a small group he was forming, but decided to stay with his regimental colleagues. He said later: 'It was one of the biggest mistakes I ever made.'

The colonel was accompanied by lieutenants Leon Blanchaert and George Lascaris, who could both speak Italian. The trio pretended to be disbanded Italian soldiers making their way to homes in the south. They were readily given permission to sleep in stables and haylofts and to gather fruit and vegetables from the fields. The officers crossed British lines at Casacalenda, north-west of Foggia, on 13 October.

In the days after the announcement of the Armistice, the Germans also targeted three POW camps neighbouring Fontanellato, with varying results.

North-west on the Via Emilia at Cortemaggiore was a little known camp for Yugoslav officers, designated PG 26. The Germans captured some of the prisoners, but there were many escapes, and several of the men became noted partisans.

PG 29 Veano, due west of Fontanellato in the province of Piacenza, held 206 officers and 62 orderlies on the eve of the Armistice. They were guarded by 150 soldiers and *Carabinieri*. The camp, in the hills between the Trebbia and the Nure valleys, was housed in the Villa Alberoni, a summer home for seminary students, 12 miles from Piacenza. It opened on 1 May 1942 for officers of field rank, majors and colonels, but more junior ones had to be accommodated following Axis successes in North Africa.

Conditions in the camp were similar to those at Fontanellato. Relations had been soured by repeated escape attempts, but not enough to prevent cooperation between the Italian Commandant, Colonel Cornaggia Medici Castiglioni, of Milan, and his British counterpart, Colonel George Younghusband. When on 10 September 1943 information was received that the Germans were approaching, 'the whole camp scattered into the countryside.' [22]

There were about 500 'other ranks' prisoners at PG 55 Busseto and its work camps. Only 10 to 15 prisoners were able to escape from the main camp, located on the plain north-east of PG 49 in the Villa Pallavicino. A British War Office summary dated 7 October 1943 said: 'The Protecting Power confirms the camp to be under German control. Escapers report that prisoners in three sub-camps succeeded in escaping and that another sub-camp was taken over by the Germans.'

A section in a notebook kept by soldier E Roberts, and now held at the Imperial War Museum, provides one of the few eyewitness accounts of what happened at PG 55:

---

[22] The story of PG 29 Veano is covered in detail in two chapters in my book, Prisoners and Partisans: Escape and Evasion in World War II Italy.

I was working on a farm for 10 weeks until September the 8ᵗʰ when Italy signed a peace. On the 9ᵗʰ a German patrol took over our camp. We moved to Mantova on a football ground. Each day Gerry was bringing in our lads who were working on farms. When the place was full, 1,300, we were put in cattle trucks on the 13ᵗʰ en route for Germany.

The satellite camps were across the River Po towards Cremona. In the summer of 1942, labour had been made compulsory for privates and lance corporals on projects unrelated to the war effort. Officers were not allowed to work under the terms of the Geneva Convention. Work detachments provided casual labour on farms and vineyards, in factories, and on building sites. The prisoners had double rations and the chance to barter items with their guards. On the Armistice, captors and captives were united in their desire to go home. Most disappeared within days.

One hundred and fifty prisoners escaped from the Busseto sub-camps and some of them were the first to cross into Switzerland. In those early days the escape routes were still open and rail traffic was not subject to adequate security controls.

On 12 September 1943 the Germans rescued the deposed dictator Benito Mussolini from what he described as 'the highest prison in the world' in the Gran Sasso mountain range. He was installed at Salò on Lake Garda and proclaimed the *Repubblica Sociale Italiana (RSI)*, a new Fascist republic for German-occupied Italy.

A week after the Armistice, the Germans issued a decree on prisoners of war. The message was broadcast over the radio, read in churches and displayed on leaflets and posters. It said: 'Anyone who gives food and shelter or provides civilian clothes to British or American prisoners will face the severest penalties before the Tribunal of War.' In practice, the sanctions included the burning down of helpers' houses, deportation and execution by firing squad.

On 23 September a proclamation offered a bounty to Italians who captured and handed over a prisoner:

> *Reward: A reward will be immediately given to anyone who recaptures British or American escaped prisoners of war. It will consist of either twenty pounds sterling or 1,800 lire, according to the choice of those who hand over the prisoner. Payment will be made by troop detachments or German headquarters to which the prisoners are consigned.*

The option of payment in enemy currency reflected the appeal of British gold sovereigns, 'the Knights of Saint George,' which were hidden under many a peasant's mattress.

On 10 October the first military decree of the new Fascist republic also made aiding and abetting the enemy a capital offence.

The response of most Italians to threats and bribes from Germans and Fascists was to redouble their efforts to help the escaped prisoners of war in every way possible.

6

Every Man for Himself

The escapers from the camps had been propelled from a life of order and routine into a dangerous and uncertain world. In addition the usual structures and discipline of military life no longer applied. It was 'every man for himself.'

The prisoners of war did not even know what the attitude of Italian civilians would be. Ian English, a captain in the Durham Light Infantry (DLI) and later chronicler of the escape from the camp, told me:

> *We had no idea what to expect. The general view was that we rather looked down on the Italians as soldiers after our experiences in the desert. Also some of us had had bad experiences in Bari and Capua camps. We were most surprised at the marvellous welcome and hospitality we received.*

The captain crossed British lines near Casoli in the Chieti province of the Abruzzo on 22 December 1943, together with fellow DLI officer Wilfred White.

The Indian Army officer Robert Williams related:

> *In company with many in the camp, when we left I knew nothing about Italians or the geography or the language. Every day it was learn, learn, learn. The local dialects in every province made it difficult to*

understand or learn Italian. Every house we went to in
Emilia and Apuania helped us in one way or another,
and we went to something over 55 places.

Captain Williams escaped to the United States 92nd Infantry Division in Tuscany on 6 December 1944. He was accompanied by one of the PG 49 medics, Captain HD Fleming, and an American airforce sergeant mechanic. The journey was organised by SOE agent Captain Charles Holland.

When I first met escapers from PG 49 I asked their opinion on the motivation of the civilian helpers. These are some typical replies: 'We understood that they had a tradition of giving help to travellers ... We were told how much they hated the government, the Fascists, and of course the Germans. We were against them too, so the *contadini* [peasants] were on our side.' (Ian English); 'I think that they helped us for humanitarian reasons, perhaps partly as a reaction against Fascism which most of them said they hated.' (Anthony Laing); 'I met frequent anti-Fascist sentiment. Many, especially small farmers, probably helped out of humanitarian reasons.' (John Langrishe); 'There was a strong anti-Fascist feeling, but in addition a number of the helpers had been in the United Kingdom before the war.' (Robert Williams).

In the vacuum after the escape from the camp, most of the men went to ground while they waited for clearer news of the rumoured Allied landings. The Germans deployed military police to search the area, but they were unable to obtain any reliable information on the prisoners' whereabouts from the locals.

After about a fortnight, German troops were brought in to search individual farms. A dozen servicemen were recaptured straight away and eventually the total grew to about 80. Two helpers were arrested and sent to the camp at Mauthausen in Austria. They never returned.

Lieutenant John Langrishe's experience in these early days may be taken as typical. He helped with odd jobs on two farms near the camp, but on 29 September was forced to flee into the fields when a German sweep began. John Langrishe recalled: 'We came to the conclusion that the neighbourhood was getting too hot to hold us and that in any case it was not right to outstay the welcome that we had enjoyed from the simple Italian farming folk.'

At dawn next day the lieutenant left, together with his friends, Captain David Buchanan and Lieutenant John Eadie, both also from the RA, and Lieutenant VA (Bunny) Buist, of the Royal Armoured Corps. It took them all day to travel 10 miles across the plain and to follow the Stirone torrent upstream into the foothills.

John Langrishe related:

> *We joined a country road running upwards and southwards along the crest of a rising ridge past some large but dilapidated houses. Looking back, we could see that even in the course of a mile or so we had risen quite considerably above the level of the plain in which we had passed the previous five months and we could also see for the first time the extent of the military traffic on the main road, the Via Emilia. On our right in a narrow valley ran a metalled highway but there was no sign of life on it with the exception of an occasional farm cart. Ahead of us rose the main ridge of the Apennines, fir-clad and sparsely inhabited.*
>
> *The day was drawing on and there was no immediate prospect of a night's shelter. Owing to the easy life we had been leading, we were all suffering in varying degrees from soreness of the feet and were extremely tired. We had already covered 12 or more miles of hard going without much food. Soon we were passing a large camp of huts among the fir trees. As we saw there were German troops moving about, we had to drive our flagging bodies yet further, for no Italian would take us in with the enemy in such close proximity. In the end, we*

finally dragged ourselves another couple of miles along the mule track we were following and entered the village of Vigoleno, nestling among the hills.

We asked for shelter at the first house and luck was with us. We were made right royally welcome and invited in by the farmer [Alberto Sanini] a well-to-do man with a prosperous looking house. In what seems less time than to tell of it, we were sitting down at a well-covered table to a magnificent supper. Our host offered a choice of a more than palatable red or white sparkling wine. When I remarked that this seemed a very fine drink, he replied that before the war it had been exported and was quite well known.

The meal over, we were taken to the house of an old couple in the village who had spent many years in England and had many fond memories of the country. They gave us an even warmer welcome, if that were possible, and a glass of excellent wine. They told us of their son who was still in England and of whom they had received no news for years. We were given messages to carry home from this heartbroken couple. Then followed the ceremony of listening to the nine o'clock news broadcast in Italian from the BBC, a custom we found had been widely observed even during the Mussolini regime despite the heavy penalties. We returned to our farm with a tearful farewell and Godspeed from the aged pair. It was in its way very touching to find Italians so pro-English.

Our bedroom was the familiar hayloft. As the night was turning cold we burrowed well down into the hay and gave our aching bones and muscles the rest for which they had been crying out for so long. The depth of our sleep proved that a comfortable bed is an unnecessary luxury if one is healthily tired.

We awoke to the sound of raindrops falling on the roof of our loft. Unless we were willing to get very wet we would have to delay our start until the weather cleared. So we took stock of our possessions as our chore before lunch...

We were given an even finer meal than that offered the night before. There was roast duck as the main course, liberally washed down with the red and white wine to which we had been introduced at supper. After lunch, as the weather had cleared, we set forth.

We had no clear and accurate line of march, mainly because the map was useless except for giving the general trend of the country. We went though Vigoleno and came out onto a side road, along which we trudged in the general direction of the hills. Progress was slowed up by the conversations we were continually compelled to make with passing Italians. We were usually taken for returning Italian soldiers of whom there were many thousands roaming the countryside. The locals were very anxious to get news of those they knew.

Because of these delays, by the time darkness began to fall we had only covered half a dozen odd miles to reach the tiny village of La Trinità, a mere handful of houses in a sparsely inhabited valley. We found the villagers very friendly and ready to help, but as they were very poor and the houses small, we were split between two families for the evening meal. We gathered afterwards to hear the wireless news...

The following morning, 2 October, dawned fine and sunny after the dull afternoon of the previous day. From the village, after a hearty farewell, we set off up a steep mule track through the chestnut forest for the village of Rigollo in the adjoining valley. Quickly we gained altitude and after a strenuous

hour of climbing we breasted the ridge to be rewarded
with a glorious view. Mountain and valley tangled
together into the blue distance beneath the cloudless
Italian sky, fir trees, mighty chestnuts, small stone
houses and red roofs. [23]

Over the next two days the escapers crossed rough country to Pieve, south-east of Bardi. Agostino Ferrari, a former chef at the Connaught Rooms in London, arranged for them to be sheltered with different families for two weeks. There were said to be two to three hundred ex-prisoners in the area. Most had decided to wait and see before attempting a long journey.

The officers decided to split into pairs. This was the best number for mutual support, while less likely to attract attention or overburden local resources. Lieutenants Eadie and Buist chose to make for Tuscany as they had heard that the cooking was the best in Italy. They reached the region, only to be recaptured and sent to a camp in Germany.

Captain Buchanan and Lieutenant Langrishe eventually also parted on security grounds, at Fano in the Abruzzo, after 42 days and 400 miles. The captain remained in the area and was liberated when the Allies arrived in 1944.

John Langrishe travelled another 130 miles and led a hazardous crossing of German lines on 19 November. His long walk out from Fontanellato to the Sangro took seven weeks and a day in 34 stages. He was Mentioned in Despatches for his actions. The lieutenant was repatriated and reached his front door in Edinburgh two nights before Christmas 1943. He rejoined the 7th Medium Regiment of the Royal Artillery in January 1944 and served with them in the north-west European campaign till the end of the war.

---

[23] John Langrishe, The Long Walk Out, pp 18-21.

Two other lieutenants from the Royal Artillery had similar experiences. Maurice Goddard told me how they left Tosca in the Ceno Valley in the third week of September:

> *We did our best to avoid all contact whilst on the move. I do not remember staying more than two nights anywhere, and then only for reasons of weather or needing boot repair. We strictly avoided keeping any record of names but did leave notes to say that we had received assistance.*
>
> *I made my way with others to the Bardi valley, then with a companion, Erik Hampson, towards Genoa in the hope that Allied forces might attempt a landing in the area. When that failed to materialise, we decided to follow the watershed of the Apennines south, hoping that our troops would quickly advance.*
>
> *We gave no thought to winter weather, nor were we equipped for it. When we reached the Abruzzo the landscape was snow-covered, which made concealment more difficult. We arrived at Opi in late November 1943, beyond which civilian movement was prohibited, so we had to travel by night. It was the only time in our lives that we encountered wolves.*

The two officers met an advance company of the Northamptonshire Regiment at Alfedena on 30 November.

The final crossing of enemy lines was when most escape attempts came to grief. Lieutenant Eric Hopkins, of the Green Howards, told me: 'I headed west for a few days on the rumour that the Allies had landed near Genoa, and then south, south-east along the Apennines.' He added that he would always remember the friendliness of the people and the help they gave: 'Having so little, they shared it with us.'

In March 1944 the lieutenant was caught near Pescasseroli in the Abruzzo mountains, together with a British POW from another camp called Freddie Swann. They managed to jump from a German lorry and a week or so later were told of a 'safe' route through the lines by an American parachutist. The pair followed it in the morning, but walked into a large force of Germans and final recapture.

Successful escape always depended on a great deal of luck. As another example, two officers out of a group of four who stayed within a day's march of Fontanellato into October 1943 succeeded. They had remained in the area for over a year. Their companions left and were recaptured. Jack Comyn wrote about the events in his book, *Episodes,* and was a great help to me in my early research. The twenty-five-year-old officer was captured by the Italians on Sofafi Ridge, just inside Egypt, on 10 December 1940. It was his first day as a tank troop commander in the Eighth King's Royal Irish Hussars.

Jack Comyn was in a group of 16 cavalry and rifle men who left the Rovacchia at dusk on 10 September 1943. It was argued that if they avoided all towns, major roads and railways, they would be certain to link up with the Allies. Landings were said to be imminent on the coast only 60 miles away at La Spezia. Jack Comyn related: 'Many months later we learned that these reports, emanating from the BBC, were put out to deceive the Germans. They certainly deceived us.'

'The first problem was to get over the railway line and the Via Emilia,' Jack Comyn told me. 'There was quite a lot of German military traffic on the road and we had to wait for intervals to scramble across. I remember some nasty wire fences. After that we just headed west into the hills in darkness and covered about 16 miles that night.' At four in the morning, Charles Hedley, the eldest, complained of foot soreness, so they laid up in a wood on a hilltop.

First light revealed a small farmhouse only 100 feet below. As Jack Comyn was judged to be the most fluent in Italian, he was sent to investigate. He found the farmer in a shed milking the cows. The man did not seem surprised at the intrusion. He listened patiently to the captain's story, and after finishing his task, filled a pail with milk and another with hot water for his footsore friend. Together they carried them up to the wood.

Towards noon, the escapers were visited by a genial landowner called Signor Palumbo. Some disbanded Italian soldiers had told them to expect 'an English millionaire.' It turned out that his million was actually in Lire, but he had run a restaurant in Soho for more than 20 years and spoke perfect Cockney. Partisan officer Giuseppe Guarnieri told me that during the war he had escorted Allied escapers to Signor Palumbo in the town of Salsomaggiore Terme.

The landowner offered to find accommodation for the men from PG 49 on local farms. They were split into small groups. Along with three other officers from the Eighth King's Royal Irish Hussars, the captain was taken to the holding of Ernesto Regalli (whom he called Regalo), just south of the hamlet of La Trinità. Aged about 30, he had a wife and two young twin daughters. Above the farm there was woodland, and below it the land dropped gently towards the Stirone, beside which ran a country road down the valley.

The party of 8th Hussars consisted, in order of seniority, of Captain Patrick (Pat) Howard Voltelin de Cleremont, Captain Comyn, newly promoted on 29 August, Lieutenant Charles Hedley, the eldest, and Second Lieutenant Donald Astley-Cooper, the youngest. Rank was still important as the men had been trained to follow the decisions of the senior officer, even in these unusual circumstances.

The Hussars were soon enveloped in the rhythm of country life, as Jack Comyn related in his book, *Episodes:*

We slept in the barn, the sweet smelling hay pleasant to the senses in those warm summer nights, and came into the farmhouse for meals and to spend the evening. The Regalo family could not have been kinder hosts. Each morning the Signora would make fresh pasta, ladling out the flour from a wooden chest onto the kitchen table, mixing and kneading it and then cutting it into strips, tagliatelle! The pasta would be cooked in the huge cauldron which hung permanently above the wood fire in the large open hearth. At the side of the hearth stood a small iron stand above a little fire of glowing charcoal. On this the sauce would be cooked using tomatoes, onions and snippets of liver or bacon. Inset deep into the thick stone wall beside the hearth was a large oven, closed with an iron door. This would be filled with a mass of twigs which would be lit, allowed to burn until the interior of the oven was hot, and then raked out. Into the oven would go freshly kneaded loaves, or sometimes a rabbit or a chicken. In the evenings our pasta would be washed down with the Regalos' own red wine, only just made and tasting abominably of the sulphur with which the vines had been sprayed.

Like all the contadini we met later the Regalos were then far from well off for food, and four extra mouths would have sorely strained their resources if it had not been for Signor Palumbo, our Lady Bountiful. Every now and then he would send up to the farm a horse and cart carrying flour, salami, cheese and wine and sometimes a chicken. His generosity was amazing, and I am glad that I was able to visit him after the war and repay a little of it. On that occasion he told me that during the war he had always anticipated catastrophe and had laid in stocks of food. He had even hidden quantities of grain in the walls of his house.

We seemed to be in no danger from the Germans. From the farm there was an excellent view of the little road down the valley, and we could soon vanish into the woods above us when a car was seen, as occasionally happened, usually Germans looking for fresh fruit and vegetables or wine. But there was a risk, feared by Ernesto, that our presence might be betrayed by a spia, a local with Fascist or German sympathies. By day we exposed ourselves as little as possible. Such diversions as we could arrange occurred after dark. Hugh Hope, who had helped me with my escape attempt at Fontanellato, was at a farm only half a mile away, together with Derek Hornsby, another 60th Rifleman, and we frequently met. At Borla, a tiny village just up the valley, there was a widow with English connections who once or twice entertained us to an excellent evening meal in her cosy cottage.

Palumbo put us in touch with neighbours of his, Manlio Carloni and his wife, a charming young couple who lived in a modern flat just outside the little town of Fidenza. They would sometimes ask us to stay, two at a time. This was quite an adventure. Fidenza lay some six miles down the little Stirone torrent. We would set off after dark, not using the road but walking down the dry riverbed. Nearing Fidenza there would be a whistle from bushes on the bank and Manlio would appear, to lead us to his home. There we enjoyed the luxury of a hot bath, excellent food and comfortable beds. All next day we would remain indoors, keeping quiet in response to Manlio's warnings that the inhabitants of the flat below were Fascisti. After dark we would return by the same route to La Trinità. Some years later I visited Manlio and his wife and was amused to receive the same injunction not to speak too loud, this time because the people below were Comunisti. I suspect that both warnings derived from nothing more than Italian love of intrigue.

One evening we were summoned to a secret meeting in a stone hut high in the woods. There we found a small party of young men all dressed in what appeared to be cowboy kit. It transpired that they were members of the dance band of a smart hotel in the spa town of Salsomaggiore, not far away. The object of the meeting was to set up a partisan group. There was a lot of talk, wine and laughter, but little was achieved except agreement for a further meeting. We turned up on the appointed evening, but they did not appear, and we never saw them again.

It was with the Regalos that I first realised how severely deficient was my Italian, obtained only from books, because I had had little opportunity of conversation. An added difficulty was that the peasants spoke only in dialect. I was later to find that the dialect varied considerably in every region, practically every valley, of Italy. Instead of andiamo a casa, let's go home, Ernesto would say andoom a ca'. And for vino [wine] he would use the French word vin. In spite of this he and I got on well and I was impressed by how hard he worked … everywhere in north and central Italy the contadini were up at 4am to start the day.

Ernesto had his little relaxations. One afternoon he beckoned to me to follow him up into the woods. He was carrying a spade, nothing unusual because there were no privies on Italian farms, all had to be returned to the land. When we stopped he dug a hole and extracted a large flagon of genuine Chianti. We spent the whole afternoon there. As he explained to me, he had sometimes to get away from the family. Ernesto also possessed a ready wit. On one occasion he was requisitioned by the local Mayor to accompany a party of German officers who wanted to shoot. A hare was wounded, and Ernesto sent to find it. He found it, but instead of delivering it the Germans hid it in a ditch. That evening we ate delicious hare stew. It was only when we had finished that Ernesto told us how he had obtained it. 'There you are,' he ended, 'that is typical of this war. The German shoots the hare, the Italian steals it, and the English eat it!'

Weeks went by, and it was now mid-October. There had been no further talk of a landing in the north of Italy, and clearly both the Allied armies were heavily involved with the Germans south of Rome. We talked of getting to Switzerland, but we knew that the Swiss were interning escapees. Wengen was not a bad place to be interned, on parole and free to ski (as many found), but internment meant taking no further part in the war. A journey through occupied France to neutral Spain might be feasible, alternatively a junction with Tito in Yugoslavia. But we now knew that we could get help from the Italians, and my inclination was to move south in the hopes of getting through to our own armies fighting there.

Pat de Cleremont did not share my view. He thought we were well off where we were and should wait further. This was awkward, as he was the Senior Officer. I sounded out Donald Astley-Cooper. He was of my opinion. One evening there was a somewhat acrimonious meeting at which Pat eventually agreed to our departure. Charlie Hedley later took me aside. 'I think you are right, Jarck,' (as he always pronounced my name) 'and I would love to come with you. But I

*might slow you up, and anyway someone must stay
with Pat.' So he did. In fairness to Pat's judgement, he
and Charlie stayed put all that winter ... After the fall
of Rome in June 1944 they were freed by the oncoming
Allies, and got home long before me.*

*Donald and I set off southward up through the
woods behind the farm. We had a map of Italy, torn
from a school atlas, somewhat lacking in detail. For the
first mile Ernesto guided us. Pian, piano [easy does it],
he kept saying, 'if you try to go this pace you will never
get over the mountains.' Then we parted.*[24]

Over the next six weeks the escapers travelled down a large
part of Italy. The journey was all on foot, apart from 30 miles by
train near Rome. The officers were given a meal and had their
boots repaired at the Franciscan monastery of La Verna in the
Casentino Forest. They also received three days hospitality from
a landowner at Ginestra Sabina called Pietro Falconi. Otherwise
the escapers relied upon the *contadini*. Every evening they would
approach a lonely farmhouse, say who they were and ask to be
received. Only on two occasions were the pair refused hospitality
in the often poverty-stricken homes. Money was never offered
and never requested. The Hussars would leave a note asking the
Allies to recognise how much their hosts had done for them.

Jack Comyn and Donald Astley-Cooper made good progress
and by 28 November had reached the battle zone on the River
Sangro. They decided to push on through the snow until contact
was made with British forces. After 24 hours the officers were
forced by mist and low cloud to seek shelter with other escapers
in a shepherd's hut. It was near Opi in the German forward
area. Suddenly there was the rattle of automatic fire and a shout:

---

[24] Donald Astley-Cooper was promoted to captain and commanded an armoured
group in Korea. He was killed on 3 January 1951 in the Battle of Koyang.

'Look out, the Jerries are coming!'

The men were recaptured and marched all day down the mountains to a POW compound. 'It was the most miserable point in my life,' Jack Comyn recalled. 'It was horrifying to find oneself a prisoner of war again after such an effort.'

The Hussars were entrained for the camp at Moosburg in southern Germany, together with many others from PG 49, including Philip Kindersley and Ronald Orr-Ewing. They served out the rest of the war in *oflags* 8F Mährisch-Trübau and 79 Brunswick, which on 12 April 1945, was liberated by the United States 9th Army. Several British officers arrived during the afternoon. Among them was gunner captain John Greenwood, who had been at PG 49 and escaped to Switzerland.

Jack Comyn left the army in 1950 with the rank of major. After three decades of farming in Ireland and Essex, he retired in 1980. Fontanellato was the only camp the major revisited. Together with his wife, Elizabeth, he was shown around by the nuns. They trod the marble stairs and agreed that it had been quite a palatial residence for prisoners of war.

Jack Comyn was able to meet his helpers once again. The farm was by then an abandoned ruin, like so many in the hills:

> *Ernesto and his wife, both much aged, had a small modern house, with a patch of vineyard, in Borla. He opened a bottle of wine, and we talked. One of the twins was married, the other a nurse in Swansea. He told me that they had looked after many other escapees after my departure. I had an uncomfortable feeling that of me he had little recollection, although he clearly remembered Hugh Hope, who had been to see him soon after the war.[25]*

---

[25] Jack Comyn, Episodes, pp 92-6.

Major Hope, a regular from Midlothian in the King's Royal Rifle Corps, related his very different escape experience:

> *I was sheltered by a farmer at Aione, near Borla. The farm opposite was raided and a Yugoslav captain captured, so I decided to leave. I was given civilian clothes by my helpers. I walked south down the Apennines from 18 October till 21 November, when I was near Castel di Sangro. During my walk I had to give my watch (a Rolex Oyster, which cost me £10 before the war) in order to get my boots resoled, the Italian refusing to accept local currency. Near Pescara I met an American parachutist officer who had been arranging the evacuation of ex-prisoners of war by sea. The scheme had come to an end by this time.*
>
> *I crossed the Sangro River near Castel di Sangro and reached the British lines at first light on 21 November. I was sent to HQ 13 Corps where I had a tactical interrogation. From there I went back on a personal visit to an officer in my regiment at Vasto. Here I met General Montgomery, who said I could stay in Italy and go to the 2ⁿᵈ Battalion of my regiment.* [26]

The general's stepson, Major Richard Carver, of the Royal Engineers, was also an escaper from Fontanellato. In December 1943 he crossed 8th Army forward positions on the River Sangro. When they were reunited, General Montgomery said to him: 'Where on earth have you been?'

[26] Escape Report in TNA: PRO WO 208/3318.

7

Through Enemy Lines

The two officers from the Eighth King's Royal Irish Hussars who decided to stay on the Parma-Piacenza border after the departure of their friends remained in enemy territory for more than a year.

Captain Patrick de Cleremont, aged 33, was educated at Harrow and Sandhurst. He was commissioned into the regiment in 1932 when it was in Egypt. The officer left the army five years later to look after his family firm of leather merchants, but rejoined from the Reserve List on the outbreak of war. He was appointed Adjutant and twice Mentioned in Despatches before his capture together with many others from the regiment at the Battle of Sidi Rezegh in November 1941. Jack Comyn had known de Cleremont before the war and described him as 'a kind and generous character, renowned in the regiment for a sardonic wit and as a bon viveur.'

Charles Hedley joined the army in 1918 and the regiment in 1921, and was to serve as a Hussar for 32 years. He was commissioned Quartermaster in the Field in June 1940 and was captured near Bir Hacheim in Libya in May 1942. A Lancastrian, described by Patrick de Cleremont as 'this little man with a big smile,' Charles Hedley was a hard worker and able administrator.

The Hussars became friendly with two Italians at La Trinità. Olimpio Dolci, aged 48, and his sister Maria, the widow of Signor Lusignani, lived together on a farm on the edge of the hamlet. Maria had brought the officers meals of pasta, bread, cheese, and wine when they first arrived in the valley. Patrick de Cleremont sent notes of thanks in French as Olimpio had worked in France before the war. In the messages, the captain referred to two officer escapers who were being sheltered by the priest of Borla, Don Angelo Lambrini, saying that it was not possible for them to join his party. It would overburden the house and the locality.

In August and September 1944 Lieutenant Hedley wrote letters confirming the help given by Olimpio and Maria, which are typical of the many thousands of testimonials that were left with Italian helpers:

> *To whom it may concern: Olimpio Dolci*
>
> *This is to certify that the above named has rendered valuable assistance to British officers and other ranks for a long period.*
>
> *He assisted me and seven other officers in September, October and November 1943 and since that time has had in his care five South African soldiers, finding them refuge during a most difficult period. He is the brother of Maria Lusignani, who is also in possession of proof of her valuable assistance to us. We hope that his work will be recognised and rewarded, as he has been a most valuable ally.*
>
> *To British or Allied HQ in Italy: Maria Lusignani*
>
> *This is to certify that the above named has rendered invaluable assistance to British ex-POWs ever since the Armistice. She has, to my knowledge, given food and shelter to a large number of officers and men who have passed through the area. The fact that she was constantly under Fascist supervision by reason of her known pro-British views has not deterred her in any*

1. The castle and square in Fontanellato.

2. The wartime prison camp 49.

3. In the grounds of the former camp.

4. The playing field - scene of escape.

5. First steps of freedom - into the plain.

QUESTA LAPIDE RICORDA
NEL QUARANTESIMO ANNIVERSARIO
I PRIGIONIERI DI GUERRA
INGLESI E ALLEATI
QUI INTERNATI NEL CAMPO
DI CONCENTRAMENTO P.G. 49
LA POPOLAZIONE DI
FONTANELLATO
CHE DOPO L'ARMISTIZIO
DEL 8 SETTEMBRE 1943
LI AIUTO' E LI NASCOSE
A RISCHIO DI
GRAVI RAPPRESAGLIE

FONTANELLATO 11 SETTEMBRE 1983

6. The tribute to the POWs and people.

7. My grandparents' home.

8. Our farm.

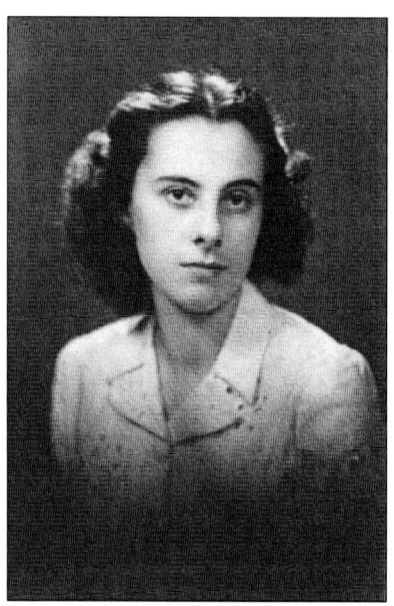

9. My grandparents before the war.

10. My mother in 1945.

11. My mother and father at San Lorenzo.

12. Lieutenant John Langrishe.

13. The Arda Valley, Piacenza.

14. The partisan's road taken by my mother.

15. La Trinità from the Stirone.

16. The escapers' hideout.

way and she has run the gravest risks in continuing her help to all who were in need.

She assisted me and seven other officers for several weeks in September and October last year.

I hope and trust that her work on our behalf will receive the recognition it so richly deserves and that she and her property will receive due consideration when British or Allied troops occupy the area.

Her door is still open at this most difficult period when so many others, for fear of reprisals, have withdrawn their assistance. She is a widow, maiden name Zoli, Zelinda Maria, and one of the stoutest hearted women I have ever had the good fortune to meet.

The Stirone Valley had been swamped by a tide of escaped prisoners of war making for the mountains. Olimpio and Maria recalled that there were continuous arrivals and departures at their house. One night, 15 escapers were given food and shelter on this small farm.

On another occasion, my mother, Clara, recalled finding a room full of excitable escaped Polish POWs in one of the houses. Some of them spoke French, as she did, and they sang the most beautiful songs. Only the silver light of dawn on the hills alerted my mother that it was time to leave.

Over a three-month period, Olimpio and Maria shared the task with three other farmers of providing food and lodging for eight British officers. In addition to the two Hussars, they included three more escapers from Fontanellato: lieutenants John Forrest Taylor and John William Burman of the Royal Tank Regiment, and Kenneth Noel Sutcliffe from the Royal Artillery. In addition, Six South African soldiers were given food and shelter for a week and food twice a week for a month. Olimpio also acted as a local guide, taking escapers across the mountains to the Ceno Valley and Bardi.

Another helper at La Trinità was Olimpio Dolci's foster brother, Pietro Guarnieri. He shared the passion for aiding escaped prisoners of war with his great friend, my grandfather, Alfredo Dall' Arda. They had grown up together in the little village of Chiavenna Rocchetta and afterwards both lived on Via Marconi in Castell' Arquato. My family was at number eight and the Guarnieris at sixteen.

Pietro was a *mediatore,* a country go-between who would arrange for the sale of anything from a patch of land to a herd of cattle. Together with a Signor Rossetti, he also rented a creamery from Olimpio at La Trinità for the production of butter and *Provolone* cheese. It was located alongside the local mill, on the gentle slopes between the Dolci farm and the Stirone. When the Germans came they stole everything.

Between October 1943 and May 1944 Pietro gave meals to those he described as *inglesi di passaggio,* 'British prisoners passing through.' He also provided money to another officer from Fontanellato, Lieutenant Costas Jacovides of the Cyprus Regiment.

At the end of the war Pietro recalled:

> *I live in Castell' Arquato but rent a small creamery at Trinità di Borla. In the very many journeys I made, I carried money, clothing and cigarettes to the prisoners. All these items were provided by friends of mine from Castell' Arquato. As a result, I also came under suspicion from the Fascist Police, but was warned in time and was able to hide.*
>
> *I gave money, bread and wine, and carried all the material provided by Mrs Filomena Scaglioni and Mr Dall' Arda. For all these reasons, I had to stay in hiding in the mountains for more than a year, because the Republicans had decided to shoot me.*

The Allied escapers in the hills included several men from prison camps other than Fontanellato. Three soldiers received help over a three-month period from five different farmers. The men were Driver Wallace H Harris, Royal Army Service Corps, from West Hallam, near Ilkeston, Derbyshire, Gunner SB Baines, Royal Artillery, and Lance Corporal R Shand, Royal Engineers, from Aberdeen.

After providing hospitality to Lieutenant Langrishe's party shortly after the Armistice, Alberto Sanini from Vigoleno gave food to the three soldiers for several days in October.

Farmer Stefano Granelli from La Villa, just downstream from La Trinità, recalled that in November and December he provided bread, milk and chickens to the three men every other day and that they lived in a wood.

His neighbour, Ernesto Varani, said that he provided Corporal Shand and Driver Harris with soup most evenings and milk in the morning. They were suffering from malarial fever and he obtained medicine to treat them. In addition, he mended their shoes and had the laundry done. The men's hideout was just across the Stirone torrent, and so in the commune of Pellegrino Parmense.

Gunner Baines spent three days with Olimpio and Maria Dolci. Driver Harris and Lance Corporal Shand were sheltered in the hayloft of Olimpio's neighbours, Antonio Solari and his wife Dina. Antonio spoke English, having worked in London before the war.

It would be nice for the story of the three soldiers to have a happy outcome, but my study of documents at Kew has revealed that they were eventually recaptured and sent to camps in Germany.

The Solaris also fed and sheltered two officers from Fontanellato in their house for 30 days over the period December 1943 to the end of March 1944. They were lieutenants William Benzie and John Burman. Four other homesteads looked after these officers in turn.

Captain de Cleremont wrote a letter confirming that Signor Solari had been of great help to Lance Corporal Shand and Driver Harris when they first came to the area. They had spent a week at their house and received food and wine. In another testimonial, lieutenants Benzie and Burman wrote:

> *Antonio Solari and his wife have fed, housed and given a bed to the two undersigned POWs from Campo PG No 49 Fontanellato. They cannot be too highly praised for their kindness and the warmth of their welcome.*

Captain de Cleremont and Lieutenant Hedley moved between farms in Vigoleno, usually travelling by night, and sleeping in haylofts and outbuildings to make it appear less incriminating for their hosts.

My mother brought the two Hussars supplies from Castell' Arquato. Captain de Cleremont sent her this letter on Wednesday, 22 March 1944:

> *Dear Signorina,*
>
> *So many thanks for the parcel of such useful things, they will be invaluable.*
>
> *It would give me great pleasure to meet you here on Sunday, April 2nd. I shall come after dark about 7.30pm.*
>
> *I hope this date will suit you. I am on my way out on a 'giro' [excursion] and shall be returning at the end of next week.*
>
> *I look forward to seeing you then.*
>
> *Sincerely yours,*
> *Patrick de Cleremont*

Other helpers included Antonio Lusci, Giuseppe Illica, a Signor Ruggi, and Miss Tina Valenta. They stayed with her for odd days over the months, and on 9 July made her farmstead their permanent base. The pair remained there till 25 October, when they began the journey south.

After three days' march, the officers linked up with a party hoping to cross enemy lines. It was led by 57-year-old Lieutenant Colonel Henry Lowry-Corry. He had been captured by the Germans at Tobruk in 1942 when commanding the 67th Medium Regiment of the Royal Artillery. After release from the senior officers' camp PG 29 Veano on the Armistice, the colonel had made his way south-west along the Apennines to Major Gordon Lett and his International Battalion of partisans in Rossano in the northern Tuscan Province of Apuania (now called Massa-Carara). The two officers had been together in the camps at Chieti and Veano, and the major found his older friend a valuable ally.

On 27 July 1944, Major Lett had been promoted to British Liaison Officer as head of the Special Force Blundell mission. Its duties were to support partisan sabotage missions, obtain supplies, assist special operations, gather intelligence, and help in the collection and evacuation of prisoners of war.

A very successful escape line, nicknamed 'the railway,' was created. It ran across the mountains, through German 14th Army positions along the Gothic Line, and on to United States 5th Army forces in the province of Lucca. The enterprise was a cooperative venture. Allied missions fed servicemen along the escape line, while the partisans provided guides and protection.

The colonel's party also included Major JE Fairleigh of the Indian Army, and Lieutenant Edward Raeburn, from the Royal Artillery. Like the 8th Hussars, he came from the camp at Fontanellato. The escapers left Rossano on 28 October. They would spend a week covering a distance as the crow flies of 51 miles in 39 hours of marching, climbing and clambering.

On 3 November the officers faced the dangerous final leg of the journey, from Isola Santa to Ruosina. Their guide, with the alias of *Baionetta* (Bayonet), turned up at a quarter to five in the morning. He wanted to pass the village and road before daybreak, so they moved off straight away down small tracks. Under a moonlit sky and in heavy rain, the escapers waded across a river and began climbing again.

The officers met other parties of escapers who tried to cut into their column, but Captain de Cleremont firmly placed them in the rear. Finally, the group grew to an unwieldy 47 people.

Colonel Lowry-Corry recalled:

> *It now became a story of mere plod, plod, plodding. Short halts occasionally when I was out of breath, but no long ones, not even ones of five or ten minutes. It rained and rained and it was too cold and windy to stand still. When daylight came we got glimpses through the clouds of other hills but my eyes were too glued to the path to pay attention. Up through the chestnuts to the beech, above the beech to tussocks of grass and stones. When I thought we ought to be getting near the top, de Cleremont told me Baionetta had just said we were half way up. My heart sank.*
>
> *We passed from rain into sleet, with slushy snow on the ground, where it could find a place to lie, and from sleet to snow. It coated our jackets an inch deep. The wind was pretty strong but not a blizzard. About a quarter of an hour after being told we were half way we reached a ridge. Visibility was only two or three hundred yards and I could not see how we could climb more unless we first went along a knife-edge. Baionetta stopped and cheered on the crowd with Su, ragazzi, su, su, morite (Up, boys, up, up, lest you die). They staggered up and as soon as all were up,*

Baionetta plunged down the other side.

At first I feared this was mere loss of height *would have to be made good again, but as we wen down, it seemed we must be over the pass, and a qu brought confirmation. It was a horrid descent, sogg tufts and loose stones, both of which gave way under one's feet and I fell more than once. Bruno came to my rescue and gave me a hand. I had no false shame about taking it.*

Then we got to marble quarries where the path was so steep that even Baionetta fell and we eased ourselves down on our seats. And still it rained. Passing over another shoulder, we were told to hurry as we were on the skyline and might be seen by [an enemy] post not far behind us.

Then we looked down into the main valley and saw villages which were in Allied hands. Several steep bits of path where wire handrails had been fixed and then we were in trees again. Still down and then a village after which we were on a main path. Cobbled and broad it zigzagged down and down and tried one's legs and feet badly. Hedley told me he felt all in but a tot of Grappa helped him on. A little later I had some too, and so did Edward, and it helped us over the last mile.

At last we got down to the riverbed having climbed not less than four thousand feet and come down the same. Crossing the river we got on a proper road. Order of march ceased to matter and the Italians pushed ahead. [27]

---

[27] The Imperial War Museum, Report by Lieutenant Colonel HC Lowry-Corry, Royal Artillery.

As the party neared Ruosina, seven miles south-east of Massa, they saw a black soldier. They had reached a forward company of the United States 92nd Infantry Division. It had taken seven hours to travel 10 kilometres.

The five officers and the guide were driven in jeeps to the battalion headquarters at Seravezza. They were taken into the guardroom and a rather apologetic Regimental Sergeant Major said that he been told to see if they could identify themselves and whether they were armed. He was satisfied when the lieutenant colonel showed his identity discs and said that he could vouch for the party. They were all taken to the mess to celebrate.

Captain de Cleremont and Lieutenant Hedley returned to England in December 1944. The following spring they rejoined the regiment in time to take part in the Rhine Crossing and the Victory Parade in Berlin.

Charles Hedley took command of the advance party of the 8th Hussars that flew to Korea in 1950 and got the best of everything for the regiment. Patrick de Cleremont commanded 'A Squadron' and was awarded the DSO for 'valiant and distinguished service.' In 1953 he took over command of the 8th Hussars at the barracks at Lüneburg. The colonel retired three years later and enjoyed country pursuits from his home on the Scottish Borders. Charles Hedley left the army after 35 years service with the rank of Major (QM) and was awarded the MBE. He retired to Southern Australia.

The story of the 8th Hussars reveals the extent to which the escapers and evaders were able to rely on help from the Italians. In the next chapter we look at the impact on the former prisoners of war and the downed airmen of the liberation struggle. It began on 8 September 1943 and only ended 20 months later in May 1945.

8

Secret Journey

At midnight on 8 September 1943 the Germans called on Italian forces in the city of Parma to surrender. The garrison was reinforced by a detachment from the 33rd Tank Regiment, which rushed from its base at Fidenza. There was also spirited defence from cadets in the infantry school. But by nine in the morning the Germans had crushed all opposition.

The province was occupied by 20,000 German troops from the 24th and Hitler SS armoured divisions of Army Group Rommel. They were soon supported by 1,600 men from the reborn Fascist state.

The area had a long left-wing tradition. The first wartime anti-Fascist public demonstration in the city of Parma was on 16 October 1942 by women demanding bread and peace. When Mussolini was deposed at the end of July 1943 his effigy had been dragged through the streets.

After the German take-over, this rebellious impulse expressed itself in the desire to help disbanded Italian soldiers and Allied escaped prisoners of war. The communes of Pellegrino Parmense, Fidenza and Salsomaggiore Terme were involved in helping escapers from PG 49 from the start.

Soon after 9 September about 150 of the men flooded into towns and villages on the plain. They received immediate assistance from anti-Fascists, who gave them civilian clothing, maps and supplies.

Gino Fantoni from the village of Parola paid for many

of the escapers to travel to the Salsomaggiore hills. They were carried in the taxi of Gino Albignani (*Canali*), who had been evacuated to Paroletta with his family. He became the driver for the Fidenza Resistance, ferrying leaders to meetings and fighters to battles.

On 20 September Lazzaro Bazzoni contacted the Fornovo Taro Liberation Committee, the CLN, and said that several fugitives from Fontanellato had arrived in Mariano di Pellegrino. The men were in urgent need of food and clothing.

One of the partisans, Luigi Sbodio, recalled that it was a difficult task to obtain money and supplies. The German threat of capital punishment for anyone providing help was on everyone's mind. However, within five days the committee had collected enough items to hand to Bazzoni for the first distribution. They even arranged with butcher Dallatomasina for the escapers to be fed on meat taken from the daily ration assigned to the German soldiers stationed in Fornovo. The help was to continue over the winter.

Following the fighting between the two former Axis partners on the announcement of the Armistice, the Germans ordered all Italian soldiers to report to their bases or be treated as deserters. At Fidenza the Germans seized remaining troops of the 33rd Tank Regiment in the castle barracks and took them to the station for deportation. However, local people and railway workers provided the captives with everyday clothing and enabled many of them to escape. Meanwhile, youths ransacked the empty barracks to obtain weapons. They were joined by other civilians looking for more everyday pickings. The angry Germans fired on the crowd in the square, wounding women and children.

Resistance in the province was initially mobilised by the Italian Communist Party, the PCI. Leaders such as Emilio Robuschi and Remo Polizzi worked tirelessly to build a network of dissidents in town and country.

On 15 October the opposition was sufficiently well organised to create a provincial CLN in Parma. It was formed by representatives of the Communist, Christian Democrat, Liberal, Republican, and Action parties.

At the end of September the PCI in Parma produced its blueprint for the partisan struggle. The Parma Valley was chosen as the sector for the recruitment and training of detachments. The Taro Valley was designated as the operational zone. Attacks would be conducted along the state highway of the Cisa and the railway line between Fornovo and Pontremoli. Finally, the Ceno Valley was selected as the district where escapers would be collected and provided with assistance so as to enable them to reach Allied forces. Guides were provided to take the servicemen to Bardi, an area with many links to South Wales through emigration. First to welcome the servicemen was the prefect, Francesco Berni.

On 23 September a meeting between Allied officers and representatives of the Anti-Fascist Committee of Parma was held at Chiesa Bianca with the aim of forming joint partisan bands, but the initiative failed. Only a few escapers joined the armed struggle.

The first partisan group was formed by students from Fidenza at S Giustina in the Lecca Valley above Bardi at the end of September. However, in mid October the band was easily scattered by Germans and Fascists and there were several arrests. Bad weather and lack of food soon ensured that the remaining youths returned to their homes on the plain.

Elsewhere in the province there were secret meetings, the spreading of clandestine literature, and acts of sabotage. In December the telephone and telegraph wires to the German HQ in Fidenza were cut. The troops fixed notices on walls threatening the severest reprisals, but the subversive activities continued.

On 8 March 1944 the first successful partisan group was created. It was named Copelli in honour of a fallen comrade.

After ambushing a *Carabiniere* car at Scipione and releasing a prisoner, men from Fidenza, Salsomaggiore and Fornovo made their base in an abandoned house at Ceriati in the Iggio Valley. Ten days later the new detachment attacked the garrison of *Carabinieri* and Forest Police at Pellegrino. It was the first firefight for most of the partisans. They also ambushed the Lugagnano-Bardi bus, which had several Fascists on board.

On 18 April the German Commandant in Fidenza issued an edict threatening the harshest penalties for spreading false rumours or engaging in rebellion. Spies were also active in the commune. A local priest, Don Lorenzo Guareschi, was denounced and imprisoned in Parma till October. His friend, Manlio Bonatti, a lawyer and member of the CLN, was also implicated. He was deported to a camp in Germany.

This spiral of partisan activity and swift reaction by the authorities made the area too dangerous for the escaped prisoners of war. On 10 April one of the orderlies from Fontanellato who had been sheltered at Mariano for four months lost his life: Trooper John Harrison, aged 27, of the Seventh Queen's Own Hussars, Royal Armoured Corps, from Belfast, Northern Ireland. Two days later an unknown Allied officer, believed to have been a Scot, fell in battle at Ponteceno.

Escapers from PG 49 who were being sheltered in the area included captains Jack Baddeley, John Fairbrass and John Moore, and lieutenants John Ballantyne, William Benzie, Richard Brooke, EJD Bruen, John Burman, FG Cook, HD (Peter) Holworthy, Kenneth Sutcliffe, John Taylor, and Jack Younger. Twelve different helpers sheltered Lieutenant Taylor in turn, including Giacomo Ziveri at Bardi, whose house was burnt down as a reprisal.

Luigi Sbodio recounted that Lazzaro Bazzoni had received alarming news from a reliable source. The Republican police had become aware that escapers were being sheltered in the Mariano area. Signor Bazzoni sent a warning note to the Fornovo Committee. The soldiers would have to leave immediately. Some of them wanted to go south-west to the mountains, either to Bardi, or to Bedonia, where he would accompany them. Others preferred to make for Milan and a crossing to Switzerland. One of the officers, Lieutenant John Taylor, of the Royal Tank Regiment, known to everyone as 'Big John,' would have to stay at Mariano through illness. He later made a successful escape.

The following evening the CLN sent a car belonging to the Lombatti Company to meet Signor Bazzoni and two Englishmen at Viazzano. The officers were driven to Fidenza Station. They were taken on board the train under the noses of Germans and the Fascist militia by hiding them among a crowd of partisans.

The authors of *Fidenza Nella Resistenza* (Fidenza during the Resistance), Aimi and Copelli, recounted that the decision to repatriate the prisoners had been made by the liberation committee of Parma. Emilio Robuschi found safe houses in Fidenza for several of the men while arrangements were made to obtain railway tickets and documents. The keenest helper was Guido Camorali, whose house was near the railway station. He was one of 72 partisan fatalities in the commune of Fidenza during the war of liberation.

Two of the escapers were tank lieutenants William Benzie and John Burman. They had been captured on 5 June 1942 during an unsuccessful counter-offensive south of Gazala in north-eastern Libya. It was the turning point of the battle. They were held in transit camp PG 66 Capua for six months, before moving to PG 17 Rezzanello and then PG 49.

The officers regularly crossed into the province of Piacenza, using the safe houses along the Stirone on the way. Several letters that Lieutenant Burman sent to my mother survive.

The earliest reads:

My Dear Miss Dall'Arda,

My friends and I cannot thank you sufficiently for the soap and cigarettes, which you have so kindly sent us. We can only say that when we return again we would be delighted to see and talk to you.

Thank you once again.

Yours very sincerely, for myself and friends,
John W Burman
Lt., RTR.

On the weekend of 8-9 April 1944 Lieutenant John Burman stayed at my grandparents' house on Via Marconi in Castell' Arquato. Next day he sent a message:

My very dear Mr and Mrs and Miss Dall'Arda,

May I place on record my sincerest thanks for the nicest and happiest weekend I have yet passed in Italy.

You cannot imagine just how marvellous it is to find oneself in pleasant and civilised surroundings after having spent nearly three years in giro [on the go].

I sincerely hope that I may repay your kind hospitality one day very soon, if not here, then at home.

Yours very sincerely,
John W Burman
Lieut. RTR

The officer also wrote to my mother on Sunday, 23 April:

Dear Miss -------,

I was sorry not to see you today, but I expect that you were unable to come because of all the trouble which took place yesterday.

However, I shall keep trying and will be at the big white stone on Sunday, May 7th at three o'clock old time.

Will you please bring with you the receipts which you wish to change and I will bring fresh ones with me, for all those which were altered or mutilated.

Also if you are able, please bring the rest of the money which you thought would be available.

Whatever happens I shall be there and I do hope that nothing occurs to stop us this time.

Please convey my kindest thoughts to your father and mother.

Yours very sincerely,
John Burman
Lieut., RTR.

The money was to finance the prisoners' escape attempts. Lieutenant Burman never did keep his appointment with my mother. He had to take swift action to avoid recapture.

The officer's Escape Report reads:

We left camp 49 under the orders of Lieutenant Colonel de Burgh and then broke up into small parties. I left the area with Lieutenant William Benzie, 42nd Battalion Royal Tank Regiment, and remained with him for the rest of the period in Italy. We lived generally in the area of Mariano di Pellegrino, Parma, for this time. We contacted the 'partisans,' whom we discovered to be

*mostly of the 'bandit' type. We had nothing further to
do with these people.*

*We were eventually put in touch with an
organisation, which after many false alarms, managed
to have us sent over the border via Fidenza, Milan and
Lago Maggiore.*

*A guide arrived at the house of Lazzaro Bazzoni
to take Captain J Moore, Lieutenant P Bruen and two
other officers to Switzerland. As these four had gone
back to the mountains for a short period, and were
therefore unavailable, Lieutenant Benzie and myself
asked to go in their place.*

*We were taken by car to Fidenza, by rail to Milan,
and from Milan to Laveno on Lago Maggiore. We
crossed to Intra and walked to Brissago with guides.
Their names were not given, nor those of the people in
whose house we passed the afternoon in Milan whilst
waiting for the train. There were two male and one
female guides.* [28]

The rail journey from Fidenza to Milan is 107 kilometres,
and Milan to Laveno, on the eastern shore of Lake Maggiore, 72
kilometres. The men arrived in Switzerland on 29 April 1944.

Lieutenant William Benzie wrote in his Escape Report:

*I was allowed to go free by the Italian Commandant. I
lived for about eight months in the district of Mariano,
Pellegrino, Province of Parma and was given food,
shelter and clothing by the people of that area.*

*I travelled by train from Fidenza on 27.4.44 to
Milan, from Milan to Laveno, crossed Lake Maggiore
to Intra. On both parts of the journey I was escorted*

---

[28] Escape Report in TNA: PRO WO 208/4243.

by a guide. At Intra I was handed over to the partisans and one of them acted as guide until I crossed the Swiss border at Brissago on 29.4.44.

I know very little of the organisation except that their work was handled by a man named Lazzaro Bazzoni, Casa Massaschi, Mariano, Pellegrino, Parma. This man did excellent work and was a tireless worker on behalf of British escaped POWs.[29]

Another officer on the journey was Lieutenant Kenneth Noel Sutcliffe, from the Royal Artillery. He had been captured on 29 June 1942. The regiment was attached to the 10th Indian Division, the main force in the Mersa Matruh fortress on the coast in north-western Egypt, which was taken by Axis forces over three days. The lieutenant was captured at El-Daba on the road to El Alamein on the last day. It was the limit of the enemy advance.

In his Escape Report he recalled:

Having received little accurate information with reference to the embarkation of our own troops I moved west into the mountainous area between Parma and Genova, until November, attempted twice to move south by secure routes but I failed to contact a reliable guide.

In January I decided to wait for an offensive to open and then to move south. On 27.4.44 an organisation with which I had been in contact since December 1943 offered a guide to cross into Switzerland. This offer I accepted due to the reluctance of the local populace to shelter me for any further length of time.

From December 1943 until April 1944 I was in contact with British lieutenants: J Younger, Coldstream Guards; J Taylor, 7th Battalion, RTR; J Burman, RTR;

---

[29] Escape Report in TNA: PRO WO 208/4241.

and W Benzie, RTR.

On 28 April, accompanied by Lieutenant J Burman, RTR, and Lieutenant William Benzie, RTR, I left Fidenza (Parma) station for Milan under the guidance of Luigi Turconi who conducted us to a private house in Milan. The same evening, we left Milan by train for Laveno on Lake Maggiore, then by ferry across the lake to Intra-Verbania. From Intra we were guided by Sergio Catallape on foot over the mountains, crossing the frontier at 17.30 hours on 29 April 1944 at Brissago.[30]

The guide on the train from Fidenza, Luigi Turconi, was a student. Lazzaro Bazzoni and his wife were shot in Milan in mysterious circumstances in March 1945.

Another of the Mariano group of escapers had succeeded in reaching Switzerland on 24 April, five days before his friends. Lieutenant Richard Neville Brooke, from the Second Scots Guards, was captured at Rigel Ridge, near 'Knightsbridge,' in Libya on 13 June 1942.

His Escape Report, unusually written in the third person, reads:

Camp 49 moved out in companies on 9.9.43 and the following night split up. Lieutenant Brooke, in company with Lieutenant JW Younger, moved to the vicinity of Pellegrino and lived in that locality till mid January, trying to get in touch with Italian partisans near Bedonia and living with them for about a fortnight and taking part in one operation which was a complete fiasco. Finding that the partisans were ineffective and unreliable, Lieutenant Brooke returned to Pellegrino and then contacted guides who took him to Switzerland by the following route: By train Fidenza to Luino, thence on foot to Ponte Tresa.

Guides from the Action Party took him by train from Fidenza to Milan and Varese, and thence in a train to a small village only a mile from the frontier. Then by foot to the wire, under the wire where a small stream ran underneath it, across a river and thence to Ponte Tresa. A very easy, practical route.

Various private organisations were heard of which appeared to operate with varying success and most of which charged large sums for taking prisoners of war to Switzerland. The best appeared to be the Action Party which was thoroughly well organised and cost nothing.[31]

The Milan section of the *Comitato di liberazione nazionale (CLN)*, the new Resistance movement, created the escape organisation in September 1943 on the orders of Ferruccio Parri of the Action Party. The *Ufficio Assistenza Prigionieri di Guerra Alleati* (The Service for Assisting Allied Prisoners of War), commonly known as the Milan Network, finally employed 359 agents, sub-agents and occasional helpers. Communists were only involved as local agents or casual operatives. Under the energetic direction of engineer Giuseppe Bacciagaluppi, the organisation helped 1,865 escapers to cross the Swiss border between September 1943 and March 1945: 1,297 from the Commonwealth, 313 Slavs and 255 other allies.

When the undertaking went smoothly it took only a day or two to transport the servicemen to the sanctuary of Switzerland. Vast sums were spent on rail travel, the purchase of cycles and boats, and the services of professional guides for the last leg of the journey, usually smugglers.

---

[31] Escape Report in TNA: PRO WO 208/4242.

Allied prisoners of war escaping into neutral territory were technically free men under International Law, but following a gentleman's agreement between the governments the Allies agreed to the Swiss exercising a measure of military control over them. The liberation of south-eastern France by the Allied 7th Army in August 1944 opened up a land corridor and allowed the repatriation of the servicemen by the end of the year.

Higher in the mountains of Parma province, the partisans were provided with weapons and supplies by Allied airdrops, which began in March 1944. On 10 June the rebels were able to occupy Bardi, the old town on a rocky outcrop at the head of the Ceno Valley. At a public meeting in the square, lawyer Giuseppe Lumia was acclaimed as mayor. An organisation was formed to help Allied prisoners of war, the *Comitato Assistenziale fra gli ex prigionieri Britannici*. In his 1945 book, *Bardi Centrale di Patriotteria*, Lumia related that 40 escapers had been sheltered in the locality.

The partisans moved down the valley and the Free Zone of the Val Ceno was inaugurated. It covered 10 communes with a total population of about 40,000. On 26 June the Free Territory of Taro was also created, based around Bedonia, Albereto, Compiano, and Tornolo. The area covered 240 square kilometres and included important road and rail links with Liguria. Achille Pellizzari was chosen as prefect and he produced a partisan newspaper, *La Nuova Italia*.

During the last two weeks of July the Germans and the Fascist *Decima Mas* launched a large-scale offensive against the liberated zones. Savage reprisals were taken against the local population: 40 civilians were executed, including three priests, and the villages of Pessola and Strela were put to the torch. Bardi was taken on 17 July.

Several officers from Fontanellato joined partisans in the province. Captain Jack Baddeley, of the Hampshire Regiment, served with a detachment on Monte Barigazzo for two months and took part in the liberation of Bardi. When the Germans retook the free zone, he moved east to Borgo Taro and for 10 weeks led attacks on the railway line. On 18 October the captain joined a party of servicemen who were escorted along the Rossano escape line. They crossed to Allied forces a week later. Jack Baddeley was Mentioned in Despatches for actions taken since leaving the camp.

Lieutenant John Ballantyne, from the Royal Armoured Corps, served with partisans at Bedonia, but became disillusioned and moved to Cereseto, above Bardi. In January 1944 he led three 'other ranks' in a bid to escape north, but they were defeated by heavy snow. The lieutenant became liaison officer with another partisan band. During the enemy summer offensive in the Ceno Valley, he was forced to go into hiding for nine days. Later John Ballantyne formed a group to collect military intelligence. At the end of October he crossed the Fifth Army front. The lieutenant was awarded the MBE for his actions.

After leaving PG 49, Lieutenant John (Jack) William Younger, of the Coldstream Guards, narrowly avoided recapture by hiding in a water tank. The 23-year-old moved to Mariano with Lieutenant Richard Brooke. They were sheltered by Lazzaro Bazzoni and Ida Papisca. As already mentioned, the officers joined a partisan group near Bedonia in January 1944, but became disenchanted following a failed attack.

Lieutenant Younger created an escape line, which successfully evacuated 18 ex-prisoners to Switzerland. One of them travelled as fireman on the footplate of a railway locomotive. The officer perfected his Italian and collated military information obtained from prisoners and partisans. His reports were carried through the lines by agents. Jack Younger finally commanded a partisan unit for a month before leaving for liberated territory. He joined SOE agent Lieutenant Commander Adrian Gallegos in a group of nine men and a woman. They reached American forward positions on 20 October. Jack Younger was awarded the MBE for his actions.

An SOE interrogating officer said in a debriefing report:

This officer was with the 31ˢᵗ Garibaldi Brigade in the district of Salsomaggiore, Parma, with HQ at Pellegrino, but had contact also with other brigades in neighbouring districts. He considered that the patriots in this sector (Apennines) are excellent fighting material, providing they have sufficient arms and equipment.

He stated also that although the Garibaldi brigades were generally considered Communist, this was not always the case. A large number of men in the brigade had no or very little Communist feeling. He stated also that the Demo-Christian party has a considerable number of followers amongst the patriots. [32]

Jack Younger returned to England and became an infantry instructor. After the war he served in Germany and Palestine and attended Staff College at Camberley. In 1949 the officer went back to Italy as Military Attaché at the Embassy in Rome. In 1970 he was promoted to Major General and concluded his military career three years later as Director, Management and Support of Intelligence. In the same year the Major General succeeded to the baronetcy.

Escapers were also able to remain in the adjoining province of Piacenza until the final winter of the war, as recounted in the next chapter.

---

[32] Interrogation Report in TNA: PRO HS 6/784.

9

From Occupation
to Liberation

Following the Armistice of September 1943 many escaped prisoners of war found sanctuary in the hills of Piacenza. The narrow valleys, deciduous woods and quiet countryside created perfect hiding places. The fugitives received spontaneous help from private individuals, local priests and members of the Resistance. In turn, the earliest partisan formations were created by escapers in a bid to ensure their survival and to avoid recapture. Rising rebel activity - including the liberation of substantial upland areas in 1944 - ensured that the province was the scene of constant fighting.

The experiences of my family were not atypical. In a twenty-month period, callers at the house at number eight, Via Marconi, Castell' Arquato, included Allied escaped prisoners of war, Italian helpers, German soldiers, their Asian allies, and British and Brazilian troops on the liberation.

In 1998 I was able to obtain copies of Allied Screening Commission files from the United States on the help provided to the prisoners of war by my grandparents, Alfredo and Giuseppina Dall' Arda, and by my mother, Clara. The documents included eight wartime letters from the servicemen. At the time, my grandfather had put the messages in dark green wine bottles and buried them in the garden at the back of the house.

The POWs had come from PG 49 Fontanellato and were still in the area at the end of March 1944.

The escapers included:

Lieutenant William Benzie, 42nd Battalion, Royal Tank Regiment, from Glasgow.

Lieutenant John William Burman, 42nd Battalion, Royal Tank Regiment, from Manchester.

Captain Patrick Howard Voltelin de Cleremont, Eighth King's Royal Irish Hussars.

Captain John W Fairbrass, 7th Medium Regiment, Royal Artillery, from Colchester.

Lieutenant Charles Hedley, Eighth King's Royal Irish Hussars, from Lancashire.

Lieutenant Costas Jacovides, 1002 Pioneer Company, The Cyprus Regiment, from Larnaca, Cyprus.

Captain John Moore, The Leicestershire Regiment.

Private William Leonard Rigby, 1st South African Irish Regiment, Union Defence Force, from Fish Hoek, South Africa.

Sub-Conductor E Victor Rolland, Indian Army Ordnance Corps (IAOC), Indian Army, of French origin.

Lieutenant Kenneth Noel Sutcliffe, Royal Artillery.

Lieutenant John Forrest Taylor, 7th Battalion, Royal Tank Regiment.

Private HJ Viljoen, Union Defence Force, from Benoni, Transvaal, South Africa.

Lieutenant André GR Willis, 4th Battalion, 11th Sikh Regiment, Indian Army, from West Moors, Dorset.

Another of the escapers was called Stanley. He was slightly older than the rest and of fresh complexion. My mother recalled that the soldier was at the house during a German roundup, a *rastrellamento*. It was a dangerous situation for everyone, but he was spirited away to the mountains. Stanley made good his escape and after the war he and my mother met up again in London.

Castell' Arquato had a German headquarters and barracks and Italian infantrymen and *Carabinieri*. Radio and newspapers churned out daily propaganda against those they called 'the traitors of 8 September' and warned of the approaching Communist menace. Film shows, dances and meetings were banned and there was an evening curfew. Identity cards had to be obtained from the town hall even to move between villages.

On the outbreak of war between Britain and Germany in September 1939, my mother took out an international subscription to *Illustrated*, a substantial Odhams publication that covered the campaign. The magazine arrived regularly from London by post every week. The last copy my mother received was dated 1 June 1940, when things looked particularly grim. Holland and Belgium had fallen and the evacuation of the British Expeditionary Force from the channel ports had begun. Italy declared war on Britain and France nine days later.

At the time of the Armistice in September 1943, my mother was a student of Foreign Languages and Literature in her third year at Venice University. She had just turned 23. In this era, most girls remained at home until they were married.

Over the months, travel to and from university became an increasing problem. The rail journey was prolonged and dangerous. People packed into the carriages, even filling the toilet cubicles and the luggage racks. In February 1944 a train taking my mother back to Venice was machine-gunned by Allied aircraft. The driver and fireman were killed. It was becoming too risky to travel between the cities, and she had to suspend her studies. In the meantime, there was the chance to give private lessons in foreign languages.

My mother jumped at the unexpected opportunity that had arisen to do something to help the war effort. She took the escaped prisoners of war money and items that were rationed or in short supply on the farms. After months in the mountains, many of the servicemen were in a sorry state. Sometimes they looked like tramps.

As someone born in London with a command of several languages, my mother was popular with the escapers and also acted, in the words of one of the partisans, 'as a point of reference' for other helpers.

Allied aircraft roamed over mountain and plain. On one occasion my mother and her Aunt Maria, another helper, hired bicycles in the village and were cycling up the valley to Lugagnano when a plane began machine-gunning the narrow road. They escaped the bullets by leaping into the ditch at the side.

Former partisan officer Oreste Scaglioni, wrote:

> *I remember your mother well as a tall and strong young girl. Heedless of the danger, she left Castell' Arquato every day with a knapsack, carrying food, clothing and news for the escapers, who were being sheltered in farmhouses in the Vigoleno area, between the Ongina and the Stirone.*
>
> *She directed the men towards Bardi, where other families who had lived in England would assist them and arrange with Don Guido Anelli and other local clergymen for their escape to Allied lines.*

The journey to La Trinità on foot takes about three hours in each direction. The route was known as the partisan's road as it was taken by so many young men leaving their families to follow the rebel cause.

The journey begins by crossing the bridge over the Arda torrent and following the right bank upstream to the hamlet of Pallastrelli. Then country trails lead over the hills facing Castell' Arquato into the little valley of the Ongina. After passing through vineyards and new plantings around the village of Bacedasco, the path climbs another escarpment, and finally takes you down into the Stirone Valley.

When we first met, Oreste told me: 'Your mother could easily have been shot. There were many Fascists in the village, and there was always the risk from spies and informers.' In a dictatorship you are even afraid of neighbours.

As well as being dangerous, helping the escapers was no simple matter. Rationing had been introduced in Italy in 1941 owing to the Allied naval blockade, but after two or three years even basics were only available on the black market or through barter.

Self-help and improvisation were the order of the day. Soap was made at home using crystals of caustic soda (sodium hydroxide) and animal fat and water. The process was lengthy, and might even be hazardous, but did produce nice mild bars of white soap.

With clothing, it was make do and mend. A local dressmaker would call at the house and in two or three days make new garments out of old. They were unpicked, turned inside out, and re-stitched.

Clothing was in constant demand by the escapers, especially as it was often wet and cold in the mountains. My grandfather sent a suit, jackets, shirts, and trousers. My grandmother would spin sheep's wool on a handloom and dye the yarn. She and my mother knitted the wool into pullovers, scarves, hats, underwear, socks, and gloves for the men. They made them handkerchiefs by cutting and hemming cotton sheets. The escapers were also provided with money and cigarettes, toothpaste, books, shoes, and wine.

Goods made from leather were virtually unobtainable. At the beginning of the war a pair of shoes could be bought for five lire. Later they cost five thousand. One pretty pair my mother bought fell apart in the rain. The sole had been made out of compressed cardboard and dyed. In the summer, most people wore wooden mules with webbing. The girls carried hammers and nails in their bags to carry out repairs. Luckily, a helper was found who had access to a store of boots that could be given to the escapers, as we shall see later.

Owing to the absence of imports, sugar had to be replaced by honey, or by sugar beet that was grown in local fields and boiled into a syrup. Chicory was used instead of coffee and an infusion of lime flowers became a substitute for tea. My mother particularly missed chocolate, a problem which was only resolved with the arrival of the Allied soldiers on the liberation. They had plentiful supplies of all the items that the Italians had been starved of for years.

Many of the farms were run on the *mezzadria* system, which dated from medieval times. The landowner, or *padrone*, provided the farmhouse, outbuildings and implements, while a *mezzadro*, or sharecropper, worked the land with his family.

The harvest and income were shared equally with the proprietor. The farmers encountered by escapers were frequently sharecroppers with a landlord living in a nearby village.

The farms were largely self-sufficient in foodstuffs. Every patch of land was intensively cultivated. The holdings produced grain, vegetables and wine. Pigs, rabbits, turkeys, chickens, guinea fowl, and pigeons were kept for the table. One or two cows lived indoors all year in stalls, and two large white oxen pulled the plough.

Wheat and wine were the main cash crops. The grain was taken to a mill and ground on giant stones powered by a water wheel, producing flour for bread and pasta, and bran that was fed to the chickens.

The grapes were trodden by foot. The juice was fermented and matured in oak barrels in the cellars, producing strong red wines, such as *Gutturnio*, and a sparkling white *Moscato*.

There was no electricity, mains water or telephones. Open fires and stoves for cooking used wood off the farms, light came from oil lamps and candles, and water was drawn from deep wells.

Such was the farm my grandparents owned, called *Bertacca*, sadly no longer ours, but fondly remembered. It stands in trees on top of one of the ridges above the village. In wartime the farm provided a panoramic view of Allied bomber attacks on the cities scattered across the plain.

The huddle of buildings was once a small hamlet. Some years ago workmen found an old inn sign in some rubble. There was also a church, which was overseen by an itinerant priest. Now its fading frescoed walls and high ceiling shelter nothing more precious than bottles of wine.

Supplies for escapers that my family were unable to obtain from the farm or the home were purchased from a shop known as the *appalto*. It was just above the arch in the old walls at the bottom of the village. The store was licensed by the government to sell salt, tobacco and tax stamps, and it also stocked a wide variety of attractive everyday necessities. My grandfather smoked a pipe and *Toscano* cigars, so my mother's purchase of smoker's requisites to give to the men did not arouse suspicion.

The young partisan Oreste Scaglioni noticed my mother's trips into the countryside to help escapers, but most people did not. Walking was the usual way of moving around, even over considerable distances. Only a few people owned a car, such as the mayor, the doctor and the vet. The roads were built for mule, or horse and cart, and had not yet been asphalted. In summer, the petrol-driven vehicles that drove along them left a plume of grey-white dust in their wake. This was still true when we visited the farm in 1958. Only 15 years earlier, the countryside had been disrupted by war.

We have already looked at the stories of several of the soldiers helped by my family in previous chapters. Fortunately, Captain Patrick de Cleremont and lieutenants William Benzie, John Burman, Charles Hedley, Kenneth Sutcliffe, and John Taylor all escaped. This is what happened to some of the others.

The two privates, Rigby and Viljoen, were amongst the 37 South African orderlies at PG 49, out of a pool of 46. They had all volunteered for the role when in other camps, eager to share what they were sure would be the high degree of comfort enjoyed by the officers.

Driver William Leonard Rigby came from Ivordor, 1st Avenue in the municipality of Fish Hoek, now part of Cape Town. He was born in 1907, worked as a bus driver and enlisted in the Union Defence Force at age 32 in 1940. The private served in the 1st South African Irish Regiment of the South African 1st Infantry Division and was captured at Sidi Rezegh in Libya. Before PG 49 he had been held on the coast at PG 52 Chiavari in Liguria.

William Rigby related: 'I escaped from Fontanellato on 9 September 1943 after the Armistice. I was recaptured on 29 April 1944 by the Fascists.' He was sent to *Stalag* 8D at Teschen, which was then in Upper Silesia in Poland. It is now divided into two towns, Cieszyn in Poland and Český Těšín in the Czech Republic. From June to November 1944 the driver was based at the work camp E579 at Niwka and mined coal.

As the end of the war approached, the prisoners and their guards made the dangerous march to link up with British and American forces in face of the advancing Russians. They reached Teschen on 17 March 1945.

William Rigby's companion, Private HJ Viljoen, was from the Transvaal, home address: 19c, Fort Steet, Benoni. Following his recapture at the end of April 1944 he was held in *Stalag* 7A Moosburg in Bavaria, Germany's largest POW camp.

A letter from the 'other ranks' escapers to my mother when they were at La Trinità reads:

Dear Miss,

We thank you very much for the shirt and the pair of pants which we have received from you. It is very nice to think that there are still people here in Italy that really care for the English. We hope that if God spares our lives that we might return this great favour you have done for us.

Giovanni and Leonardo

P.S. Mary [Dolci] told us that if we need anything we must write and ask you. We need these things:
Two shirts, two hats, two pairs socks, soap, handkerchiefs, cigarettes, two jackets, toothpaste and brushes. These are all the articles we need, if they can be found.

Three of the officers were recaptured. Lieutenant André GR Willis served in the 4th Battalion of the 11th Sikh Regiment. It was the most highly decorated unit in the Indian Army and fought in the Middle East and North Africa and later in Italy. The lieutenant was imprisoned at *Stalag* 7A Moosburg. So too was Captain John Moore of the Leicestershire Regiment. Captain John W Fairbrass, from the Medium Regiment of the Royal Artillery, was held in *Oflag* 7B Eichstätt, which was also in Barvaria.

Another officer, Costas Jacovides, was a Greek Cypriot from Larnaca. He was promoted to full lieutenant at nearby PG 41 Montalbo. The officer served in 1002 Pioneer Company of the Cyprus Regiment, which was raised as part of the British Army in 1940 and disbanded in 1950.

As recounted in my book, *Prisoners and Partisans: Escape and Evasion in World War II Italy*, when the encampment on the Rovacchia broke up on 11 September 1943, Lieutenant Jacovides volunteered to work on a local farm, together with his friend from Montalbo, Second Lieutenant William John (Jack) Frank Clarke, of the Royal Army Ordnance Corps. The first holding was not to their liking, so they went to lodge with the local district nurse, Signorina Bianca Gelati, until she found them a new billet. It was the farm of the Gotti family at Cannètolo, a little hamlet to the west of Fontanellato.

The officers stayed from 16 to 27 September, helping the farmers to harvest beetroot and Indian Corn. Then German raids on surrounding farms prompted Jack Clarke to decide to leave the area. In contrast, Costas Jacovides wanted to stay and wait for the British to arrive.

Jack Clarke found two new companions, the Fontanellato dentist, South African Captain Marcus Kane-Burman, and one of his acting technicians, a Royal Navy rating, A McLean. They began the long trek south to friendly forces.

The trio were recaptured within sight of Allied positions on the River Sangro on 19 November. The officers managed to jump from a prison train near Orte on 5 December, but became separated. After many further adventures, Jack Clarke escaped to Switzerland on 24 February 1944, together with fellow forty-niners, Lieutenant Anthony Laing, Royal Engineers, and Captain Ted Mumford, 3rd. Gurkha Rifles.

Captain Kane-Burman was recaptured in Rome on 8 January, but escaped from another prison train as it crossed into Lombardy. On 1 March he also reached Switzerland. The captain became Chief Dental Officer to the large Allied escaper and evader community. On 1 March 1945 he was awarded the MBE for services to his fellow prisoners of war in Italy.

Lieutenant Jacovides adopted the alias of *Mario* and moved to the Arda Valley. He was helped by several residents of Castell' Arquato and by Angelo Istroni and family at Lugagnano, three miles higher up the valley. They also owned a mill (now derelict) on the opposite bank of the Arda, near the hamlet of Pallastrelli.

One of Angelo's granddaughters, Silvana Ghezzi, told me:

Mario stayed at the mill of follo, which belonged to the family of my maternal grandmother. When it became too dangerous a hiding place, both for him and the mezzadri who had looked after him, my family decided that he would be safer at my grandmother's house in town. She lived at Lugagnano in Via Matteotti, a short distance from the Carabiniere barracks. Mario always wrote to my aunt Adriana, who, I am told, was then an attractive 17-year-old, of whom he had become fond. But the person who looked after his safety was my mother Livia Istroni. Among other things, she was a partisan courier under the name of Katusha.

Among Lieutenant Jacovides's helpers in Castell' Arquato was Signora Alba Sebastiani. A high school gymnastics mistress, aged 30, she was a widow, with a three-year-old-son called Franco. In 1938 the teacher had married naval lieutenant Agostino Angeloni, a submariner from Genoa, but he was lost on active service. The house was number 130 on Via Sforza Caolzio, the small road that winds to the top of the village. The teacher recalled that Lieutenant Jacovides arrived at Christmas 1943 and stayed for a total of 10 days in two visits.

Over the next eight months Alba also took the officer items when he was at the mill at Pallastrelli. They included woollen pyjamas, an elegant shirt and an angora pullover, cigarettes, butter, wine, liquors, cakes, honey, tea, sugar, and bars of soap. She added: 'I also helped the lieutenant by placing myself in danger to ensure that he was not captured. I accompanied him whenever he had to go out, as the authorities were looking for him.'

After leaving the teacher's home, Costas Jacovides came to stay with my family for 10 days at the house in Via Marconi. Then on 17 January he wrote a letter to Alba, saying: 'On the orders of

Signora Scaglioni [see below] I have to leave the place where I am at present.' He asked for help for two or three days till he found out more about conditions at Lugagnano.

Signora Emma Pollorsi, then a teenager, related that Lieutenant Jacovides lodged with her and her mother, Filomena, for about a month. They were also hiding an Italian soldier. The house at 12, Vicolo San Pietro, is in a little lane just off the main road, in the oldest part of Castell' Arquato.

She recalled:

> *He often showed me a photograph of a lady with a baby*
> *who he said was his sister. He also talked about Cyprus,*
> *and spoke Italian well. As long as he remained with us,*
> *he was treated as one of the family.*

Eventually it became too dangerous for Lieutenant Jacovides to remain in Lugagnano. The barracks was hit by fire, and the wall of the Istroni house nearby developed large cracks. In September 1944 Livia took 'Mario' to a new refuge at Castelletto, a small village beyond the dam on the Arda at Mignano. A note to Adriana from Lieutenant Jacovides on 25 October said that he was leaving for the Pelizzone Pass, where he would rendezvous with three other prisoners of war. Their escape through the lines was under way.

The president of the Cyprus Veterans' Association WWII, Mr Loizos Demetriou, told me:

> *On his return to Cyprus, Costas Jacovides rejoined*
> *the Cyprus Regiment and served until the end of the*
> *war, reaching the rank of major. After his discharge*
> *from the Army he lived and worked in his hometown*
> *of Larnaca.*

Signora Filomena Scaglioni was a major benefactor of the prisoners and partisans. She lived in a flat on the second floor of the block overlooking the market square at the bottom of the village. It was 80 yards from the German barracks. Every few days my mother and Pietro Guarnieri would call on Filomena, a lively well-to-do lady. She was the daughter of an elderly shoe factory owner and widow of Signor Marchi. Over a glass or two of cherry brandy the trio would discuss their efforts to help the escapers.

One of the former prisoners of war, Yugoslav lieutenant Jovan B Grkavac (known to everyone as *Giovanni lo Slavo*), partisan commander of the *62ⁿᵈ Brigata Luigi Evangelista*, recalled that 'Filomena freely gave clothes, boots, money, and food to whoever asked for them.' The assistance was provided in a large area between Castell' Arquato and Lugagnano where there were very many escapers. Among those who received help were 'Captain *Patrizio* de Cleremont and his group of English POWs,' Prince Don Alfonso de Liguori, who was a civilian internee with South African nationality, and several fellow Yugoslav officers. Filomena's aid was usually consigned to the prisoners in the mountains through Pietro Guarnieri or Signorina Rosa Manzi of Lugagnano.

Filomena Scaglioni's nephews, Oreste and Augusto, were both partisan officers. Their stepfather, Raffaele, was an Italian army lieutenant colonel. He was captured during the German takeover of Parma and deported to a concentration camp. Towards the end of September 1943, his wife Valentina and the two boys became evacuees at the apartment of the paternal grandparents in Castell' Arquato. The flat was near to that of Filomena. For 10 to 15 days the family hid an escaped prisoner of war, probably 'Mario,' Lieutenant Costas Jacovides.

Oreste was called up by the Fascist Republic in October 1943, but instead left to join the partisans in the mountains. It was there that he met the escaped prisoners from Fontanellato. In August 1944 Oreste transferred to the Valdarda Division and in March the following year became liaison officer at the zonal command at Groppallo in the Nure Valley. His younger brother, Augusto, aged 19, guided escaped prisoners of war from PG 49 into the mountains after the Armistice and took part in student protests against German occupation. He joined Oreste as a partisan in June under the name of *Flavio*. Following combat against the Germans during the summer roundup, Augusto was made leader of a new detachment. He fell in action on 4 December at the Pass of Guselli while opposing the enemy occupation of Morfasso.

In the first months of 1945, Signora Scaglioni was obliged to flee the village after threats from the Fascists that she would be shot. At the end of the war, the Allied Screening Commission recommended her to the British War Office for the Award of Commendation (Certificate 17), 'for services rendered to the Allied cause for approximately one year,' but as usual only the Alexander Certificate was awarded.

Twelve of the 17 British Commonwealth prisoners of war helped by Filomena Scaglioni were ones who also received assistance from my family. The others were: South Africans: Lance Bombardier HC Van Biljon and Private J Freedman, and Britons: Driver G Bicknell, from the Royal Army Service Corps, Private TL Kenyon, of the Sherwood Foresters, and Guardsman J Dinsmore, from the Irish Guards.

The two South Africans and Private Kenyon were sheltered in Lugagnano for a long period. They are believed to have later crossed the lines. In contrast, Driver Bicknell and Guardsman Dinsmore were recaptured and sent to camps in Germany.

The departure of many of the POWs along escape lines in late 1944 was fortunate. In a radio proclamation on 10 November General Alexander said that owing to the weather no major attack would be launched by the Allies until the spring. The partisans were to cease from engaging in large-scale operations, conserve all stores of ammunition, and await further orders.

The announcement was seen by German and Fascist forces as an invitation to launch attacks on partisan-held areas across occupied Italy. At the end of the month they invaded the Apennine valleys. The force consisted of three regiments of the new Italian *Bersaglieri* Division and 5,000 legionaries from the German 162nd Infantry Division, often known as the 'Turkoman Division.' It was the largest of Hitler's Eastern Volunteer Formations, created from captured Soviet prisoners of war and refugees. The division was led by German officers but composed of Turkmen and Azerbaijanis. They were always known to the Italians as *i mongoli*, or the Mongols.

The troops overran the partisans in three of the four main Piacentine valleys, the Tidone, Trebbia and Nure, by 2 December. They had made a rapid advance of almost 100 kilometres from across the plain, but then suddenly stopped on the edge of the Arda Valley.

Research associated with the production of the book, *La Resistenza in Val d'Arda*, by partisan commander Giuseppe Prati discovered the explanation. The War Diary of the German 14th Army revealed that the 162nd Division met such stubborn resistance between 23 November and 2 December that many detachments needed reorganising owing to heavy losses.

Over the next five days the Valdarda partisans also conducted successful counter-attacks at the entrances to the valley, with the help of some fighters from the Nure. The enemy were forced to halt on their positions for a month.

In early 1945 the offensive resumed. On Twelfth Night, when snow was three foot deep, a force of 15,000 Italian and Asian troops launched the largest ever roundup in the border area. The republican forces included the *Bersaglieri*, *Littorio* and *Decima Mas* divisions, as well as the Black Brigades and the Italian SS.

It was the first time that villagers had seen the Mongols, as my mother related:

*It was New Year and there was heavy snow. I was
with my mother and father in one of the fields just
along the road past our house. A neighbour had
said that we could gather some sugar beet to make
our sweetener.*

*Suddenly a long column of Mongol troops began to
emerge through the gloom. They had come from the San
Giorgio direction and were going into the village. The
soldiers rode on horses and sledges and wore furs. They
had inscrutable expressions and long moustaches. It was
like a scene from the Russian steppe.*

*Before long, the Mongols began to call at our house,
looking for food and drink. I think they were based just
around the corner at the San Carlo inn.*

*My father was hospitable to everyone, so once
the soldiers had shown that they were no threat to
us, he made them welcome too. Fortunately, we had
plenty of provisions from the farm. As usual, the wine
flowed freely.*

*The Mongols gained a fearsome reputation when
fighting the partisans, but we found them gentle, almost
child-like. They said my father was their father, my
mother was their mother, and that I was their sister.*

Soon Germans were billeted with local families, as my mother
recalled:

*We were very alarmed when the troops came to the door.
But fortunately they only wanted rooms. On the whole
the Germans acted in a proper manner and got on with
their own affairs. They didn't take any of our food, for
example. It was said that the men were well behaved
because their headquarters was in the village.*

The soldiers were pleased to discover that I spoke

German and I used to converse with one or two of them. I remember they wanted more space and told me that I should go and sleep in my mother and father's room, but I refused.

The Germans occupied the main room, the sala, on the ground floor. I couldn't stop thinking of the escapers sitting on the settee talking to us there a few months earlier.

We were very pleased when the Germans went after about six weeks. They left some empty plastic containers used for processed cheese, and it was the first of the material we had seen. It was all celluloid with us.

The sala had a fine marble tile floor and hand decorated gold leaf on the walls. We discovered that the soldiers had caused some damage and had kept rabbits in the room to supplement their rations.

Some people said that the Germans were not too bad. Those they had met seemed to be very ordinary and pleasant and intelligent enough. But a youth from the village who went to Venice University with me was executed by German troops for no reason. His family were not allowed to bury his body. I also lost my second cousin, a young partisan fighter.

On Thursday, 5 April a column of German and Fascist troops launched a dawn attack on Castell' Arquato with the intention of demolishing the bridge over the Arda, and severing links to Fiorenzuola and the Via Emilia. As soldiers began to lay charges under the arches, they were hit from several different directions by fire from partisans of the 38th and 62nd brigades, armed with mortars, machine guns and light weapons.

The saboteurs abandoned their dynamite, and the column splintered. Fighting spread along Via Marconi and into the garden of my grandparents' home.

As bullets began to whiz about, my grandfather boiled olive oil on the stove to throw over any of the Germans rash enough to enter the house. Fortunately for both parties, none tried. The partisans captured two armoured cars and took many prisoners that day. The bullet holes left in the walls of the house impressed me a great deal as a boy.

The Allied offensive resumed and culminated in the Battle for the River Po. On Saturday, the 21st, the Fifth Army liberated Bologna, the capital of Emilia. German forces had fled from Fontanellato three days earlier.

The advancing troops reached Parma on the evening of Wednesday, 25 April. Next day the 62nd Brigade of the Valdarda partisan division made contact with the United States 93rd Division at Alseno. German troops scrambled to cross the river. Almost a million were forced to surrender.

My mother and her friends walked to Fiorenzuola to join jubilant crowds cheering the Allied troops as tanks and infantry advanced along the Via Emilia. The girls threw the soldiers flowers and gave them bottles of wine.

British and American forces took the city of Piacenza, assisted by the partisan formations of the valleys, on Saturday, 28 April.

All German and Fascist forces in Italy surrendered on Wednesday, 2 May 1945 following 20 months of war in the country. The celebrations began.

1 0

After the War

In peacetime, the building next to my grandparents' home in Via Marconi in Castell' Arquato, the *Consorzio*, or agricultural cooperative, became the barracks for soldiers of the victorious Brazilian Infantry Division.

The soldiers were invited to a party at the house to celebrate the liberation. In the front room there was a handsome veneered Philips radiogram, a combined radio and record player. During wartime my mother would walk down from the farm on summer evenings to listen to the latest news on the fighting from Radio London and return after midnight. Now the radiogram was used to play records to accompany the Foxtrot. It was time to dance. It must have been a good party, because relatives and friends still remember it today.

My mother decided that she would like to work for the Allied Military Government and called at the provincial headquarters, which was located in the Gothic Palace in the centre of Piacenza. After a short interview she was employed as the interpreter for the Governor, a very pleasant American, Major Lewis J McIntyre.

While lodging in the city my mother met her future husband, my father, Kenneth Winston Tudor, from Newtown in Mid Wales, who arrived with the Eighth Army. He was a regular soldier in the Royal Corps of Signals and veteran of the evacuation of the British Expeditionary Force from France in 1940. There too the order had been given: 'Every man for himself.' In the summer of 1943 my father embarked at Greenock for the voyage to Sicily. He was in the first wave of the invasion force that came ashore from landing craft on 10 July.

Two years later my father was a Quartermaster Sergeant in the Third Railway Telegraph Squadron. He was 26 years old. The section consisted of about 65 men, who were split into small detachments. They worked alongside various other Commonwealth nationalities, Poles and Americans. The first task was to replace the telephone wires along the main railway line from Piacenza to Parma, which had been destroyed by Allied bombing.

Towards the end of 1945, my mother bought glass baubles and trimmings in Piacenza and invited my father and his two close friends from the corps, Signalmen Hugo Rees and Bill Hannon, to join the family for an English-style Christmas. Hugo told me: 'Your grandfather was a big, jovial man and he treated us all like part of the family. He was so kind to us. We hadn't had a home Christmas for three or four years, but it was all over in a couple of days, sad to say.'

My father completed his continental army service in Villach in Austria and returned to civilian life in 1947 following more than eight years with the Colours. With another four years in the reserve, he became a rural postman and then a post office telephones linesman and foreman.

For a time my mother went to work in Rome. She learned shorthand and typing and became secretary to a relative, Italian army colonel Alberto Inzani, aged about 60, who was originally from Vernasca. My mother then trained as a teacher before returning to her beloved London in 1947 as a governess with a doctor's family. Her mother and father gave her the money for the fare from the payment received from the AMG for helping the prisoners. My parents married in Swindon, Wiltshire, in February 1948 and settled in Newtown.

Grandfather Alfredo never returned to London. Foreign travel was far less common except for reasons of war or economic necessity, and he was very happy in the village.

In contrast, in later years, grandmother Giuseppina made regular trips to Mid Wales to visit her daughter, son-in-law, and the two grandchildren: me and my sister, Monica. In the early 1960s she came to live with us at our home, Breeze Hill in Newtown. The house on Via Marconi in Castell' Arquato was sold, as was the farm *Bertacca*. With the abolition of the *mezzadria* system in 1964 many such holdings became uneconomic for their owners, and a traditional way of life was lost forever.

Over the next few years, my grandmother bought a flat in Castell' Arquato for occasional visits, and two more as investments, one in Fiorenzuola and the other on the coast at Imperia. But gradually the capital dwindled and finally the decision was made to sell everything. Within a few months my family became visitors and no longer residents.

Over the years, I have visited many of the towns and villages in the Emilian countryside whose people showed such solidarity with Allied escaped prisoners of war and downed airmen.

The former camp at Fontanellato, PG 49, is now the *Centro Cardinal Ferrari*, a private hospital. It is named after a famous local priest, Andrea Ferrari, who became Cardinal Archbishop of Milan. During the First World War he sponsored charities in aid of widows and orphans, relatives of those missing in action, and prisoners of war. The Cardinal was beatified by Pope John Paul II in 1987.

As we have seen, after the Allied prisoners of war escaped in September 1943 the camp was ransacked by both German troops and Italian civilians. Later the building was used as a school for officer cadets of the Fascist republic, the RSI. At the same time, the castle in the village centre was a German Headquarters. As a result of these strategic targets, Fontanellato was hit several times by Allied bombers.

In 1948 the Children's Home of the Madonna of Fontanellato

finally opened. At its peak it housed 250 orphans and 23 sisters, just less than half of its complement of prisoners of war. The orphanage closed in 1982 when new regional arrangements were made.

On railings to the left of the main gateway there is a metal panel, which reads:

> *This plaque records, on the fortieth anniversary, the British and Allied prisoners of war who were interned here in prison camp PG 49 [and] the people of Fontanellato who after the Armistice of 8 September 1943 helped and hid them at the risk of severe reprisals.*
> *Fontanellato, 11 September 1983.*

What happened to the more than five hundred officers and men who marched out of the camp at midday on 9 September 1943? The first United States officer sent to help with official rescue work in the south of Italy, Captain Richard Lewis, reported in October 1943 that: 'The opportunity of rescuing really large numbers of prisoners had already been lost when the Armistice was announced.' There were always going to be far more recaptures than successful escapes.

So it was at Fontanellato. A large majority of the prisoners were eventually rounded up and sent to camps in Greater Germany. They remained behind the wire until liberated at the end of the war in May 1945.

Some of the escapers were shot by Germans and Fascists, and others perished in severe weather. A few were never heard of again, contributing to almost 2,000 former prisoners of war in Italy still reported as missing in 1947.

On the other hand, perhaps as many as a fifth of the forty-niners made successful escapes, divided roughly equally between those who reached Switzerland and the rest who crossed Allied lines within Italy. I am pleased that my family helped some of the men on their way.

I recently revisited La Trinità, the first port of call for many of the prisoners of war from PG 49, together with my two ex-partisan friends, Luigi Sesenna and Mino Avogadri.

The village is on a hillside overlooking the left bank of the Stirone. A collection of houses and barns, a small church and an inn hug the contours of the winding country road. The turrets of Vigoleno castle peep between the hills further down the valley.

In a dip just below the village, the mill and the cheese factory (run by Pietro Guarnieri and his partner Rossetti) have long since gone, replaced by a large modern villa. The old mule track to Borla along which the servicemen trudged towards the mountains has now been widened and asphalted.

This is a hunting area and the escapers always commented on the barking of dogs that followed them from farm to farm. Wherever we walked, we attracted the attention of their noisy descendants, who were tethered on long chains.

In wartime there were only a few houses. Many new ones have been built and the older ones restored, often by returned emigrants. The people are fewer though, owing to the drift to the cities. Many buildings have become second homes, even if the owners frequently have local connections.

We called in at the inn, which is well known in the area for its good food. When I told our story and mentioned the helpers, the lady proprietor said that Antonio Solari was her uncle and that she lives in Olimpio and Maria Dolci's old house.

The dwelling, which my mother visited regularly with money and supplies for escapers, stands on a curve at the top of the village. It was damaged at the end of the war and had to be substantially rebuilt.

The restaurateur recommended that we see her relative Gino Rizzi, still a cattle dealer at 87, who is Dina Solari's brother. Gino served in the *Alpini* during the war, but as he was the only son was stationed at Piacenza instead of on the border at Bardonecchia, and so saw what was going on at home.

After a good meal at the inn, we heard stories of the wartime escapers and then walked to the opposite end of the village where they had been hidden in the abandoned house at the top of Gino's field. It is said to be the oldest dwelling in La Trinità.

As in wartime, the building is divided vertically into two unequal sections. One part is owned by Gino and the other by his neighbours on Antonio and Dina Solari's old farm. The couple's farmhouse has been replaced by a large new one with spacious outbuildings.

The families on the farm and the surrounding houses came out to talk to us. They offered us something to drink. 'You see what good people they are,' said Luigi. 'Without their help during the war, our cause would have been lost.'

The farmers readily agreed to show us the hiding place. We plodded past ancient apple trees in blossom, the rich dark earth sodden underfoot after rain.

During the war the upstairs of the abandoned house was a hayloft. A wooden ladder was used by the escapers to gain access to the top floor, which they would pull up after them. Wine was stored in the cool of the basement.

The soldiers would join the farmers for meals in the evening, and many a boisterous hour was spent in talking about the war and happy times to come.

At Easter-time in 2009 I again set out with my two friends, Luigi and Mino, to follow further lost trails. When discussing with Major Comyn the little house on the Stirone where he and his three friends had been sheltered after they left the camp, I always had the feeling that it might have been one of those my mother visited.

The farm was south of the river and abandoned. Could we locate it and find out more? We travelled by car up the Stirone Valley, along the main road from the plain.

The innkeeper at Borla told us that Ernesto Regalli's son

Claudio had been in that very morning and that we might be able to find him on his land across the valley. We followed the friendly host's directions and drove along the right bank of the Stirone to a point about 600 metres upstream of the bridge at La Trinità.

We were delighted to see a figure wearing an anorak and baseball cap, who was tilling the soil in the pouring rain. We introduced ourselves and told Claudio of our quest. He climbed into Mino's Volkswagen to talk in the dry.

Claudio, in his early sixties, has the weathered complexion and firm handshake of a countryman. He told us that the family farmstead was sold years ago. It has been replaced by the impressive villa a hundred metres above us on the hillside, which was built for people from Milan. He has retained the land between the road and the stream, where he cultivates an orchard and grows vegetables.

Claudio added that as well as his father and mother and four children, the farm had been home to his mother's parents and her sister. His grandfather, Partemio Solari, had been a restaurateur in London before the war, like my grandfather, and so was able to talk to the escapers in English.

I had been trying to discover the identity of a farmer with this very Christian name for over a year. Family friends Giulia and Emma Guarnieri told me how they accompanied my mother through La Trinità and down across the Stirone to take supplies to a farm where two escapers were sheltering. The route was via Monte Ciocca, except once when there were Germans there. The girls had looked for the men after an enemy roundup, but they had disappeared. The farmer's name had been Partemio.

Claudio also revealed that his aunt, who is called Eva and now lives in Germany, had married one of the escapers that his family had sheltered on the farm. He was Sub-Conductor Victor Rolland, a warrant officer in the Indian Army who was of French origin. Like most of the escapers in the area, he too had come from the camp at Fontanellato.

I knew the name well. Victor was one of the prisoners with whom my mother was in regular contact, and my grandfather had provided him with a suit and other items. This is an early letter the soldier sent to my mother from the farm:

> *Dear Miss C.,*
>
> *I thank you very much indeed for the so useful articles which I have received from you: handkerchiefs, smoker's outfit, combs, and the bottle of vino, etc. All at a time when I did happen to be in need of those very things. They have been very much appreciated I assure you.*
>
> *Yours gratefully,*
> *Vittorio.*

Claudio told us that Victor had managed to avoid recapture and remained in the area. After the war the happy couple went to live in Wales.

With our thanks ringing in his ears, Claudio got out of the car and returned to his land and the rain. As we sped off towards the main road, I conjured up an image of the escapers, my mother as a student, and the other helpers in this quiet, little valley. The spell was broken by Mino asking: 'Would you like to go back to Castell' Arquato, or directly to Fiorenzuola railway station?' I was returning to Milan that night. If only things had been so simple all those years ago.

Resources

1. The United Kingdom National Archives

The National Archives, Kew, Richmond, Surrey, TW9 4DU.
Website: www.nationalarchives.gov.uk

The Archives holds numerous records on British and Commonwealth Prisoners of War during the Second World War. It also provides Military Information Research Guide 20, *Prisoners of War, British, 1939-1953.*

a. Awards to Civilian Helpers

The files in WO 208 include recommendations for honours and awards to Italian civilians and military personnel who assisted Allied escapers and evaders.

b. Escape Reports

The post-Armistice reports in WO 208 were made by escapers who crossed Allied lines in Italy or travelled north to neutral Switzerland.

c. Liberated Prisoner of War Interrogation Questionnaires

Liberation Questionnaires in WO 344 were completed by approximately 140,000 British and Commonwealth servicemen and some other Allied nationals and merchant seamen.

d. Nominal Lists of Prisoners of War

   (i) The listing in WO 392 includes prisoners of all services and the merchant navy held in Italy until August 1943.

  (ii) Three books in the Resource Centre and Library provide alphabetical registers of approximately 169,000 British and Commonwealth POWs in Germany and occupied territories.

      a. *Prisoners of War, British Army, 1939-1945.*

      b. *Prisoners of War, Naval and Air forces of Great Britain and the Empire, 1939-1945.*

      c. *Prisoners of War, Armies and Other Land Forces of the British Empire, 1939-1945.*

The books include details of name, rank, service or army number, regiment or corps, prisoner of war number, and final camp location.

e. Prisoner of War Camps Reports

The reports in WO 224 were made by delegates and representatives of the International Committee of the Red Cross (ICRC), or by those of the Swiss Government acting as the Protecting Power, the neutral state which represented the interests of the Allies in Italy.

    The prisoner of war camps in Italy were identified by a serial number after the abbreviation PG, for Campo di Prigionieri di Guerra (camp for prisoners of war). Work camps were distinguished by a subsidiary number. For example, PG 55/4 was the detachment at Stagno Lombardo under the main 'other ranks' camp of Busseto, Parma.

    The extension, PM, for Posta Militare, or Military Post, and a four-digit number, provided information on the district in which the camp was located: North-western Italy was 3100, Northern Italy, 3200, Central Italy, 3300, the Naples area, 3400, and the rest of Southern Italy, 3450.

2. The United States National Archives & Records Administration (NARA)

8601, Adelphi Road, College Park, MD 20740-6001, USA.
Website: www.archives.gov

Records of Allied Operational and Occupation
Headquarters, World War II.
Record Group 331:
331.23.1 Records of the Allied Screening
Commission (Italy).

3. Other National Archives:

a. Australia - National Archives of Australia
www.naa.gov.au
Australian War Memorial, Museum and Archive
www.awm.gov.au

b. Canada - Library and Archives Canada
www.collectionscanada.gc.ca

c. New Zealand - Archives New Zealand
www.archives.govt.nz

d. South Africa - National Archives and Records Service
www.national.archives.gov.za

Note: Italy does not have a 'National Archive' but a system of more local repositories. There are various archive offices at regional, provincial and communal levels.

4. The International Committee of the Red Cross

International Committee of the Red Cross (ICRC),
Archives Division, 19, Avenue de la Paix, CH 1202 Geneva,
Switzerland.
Website: www.icrc.org

In September 1939 the ICRC set up the Central Prisoners of War Agency at Geneva in Switzerland. The warring nations also created National Information Bureaux, as required by the 1929 convention. These liased with the agency on POW matters and exchanged lists of names, messages, and news on individuals. Data on enemy prisoners of war held in Italy was obtained from the official lists, Red Cross capture cards sent by the men themselves, and enquiries conducted in the camps by the ICRC inspectors.

The Tracing Section of the ICRC Archives may be able to provide information on a person who was held as a prisoner of war or as a civilian internee during the Second World War. Research is conducted free of charge when requested by the individual or their family, otherwise an hourly fee is payable. An online form is available. The Archives replies to requests within six months. The information is provided in the form of an attestation containing everything known to the ICRC about the person concerned.

5. The Anglo-Italian Family History Society

Website: www.anglo-italianfhs.org.uk

6. The Imperial War Museum London

Lambeth Road, London SE1 6HZ.
Website: www.iwm.org.uk

7. Ministry of Defence

Website: www.mod.uk

The site includes research links and one to the Veterans-UK website.

8. The Monte San Martino Trust

Flat 7, 18, Lambolle Road, London NW3 4HP.
Website: http://msmtrust.org.uk

The charity was founded in 1989 by J Keith Killby, together with other former prisoners of war in Italy. It awards English language study bursaries to Italians aged 18 to 25, in recognition of the courage and generosity of the Italian people who aided thousands of escaping Allied prisoners of war.

The Trust relies largely on donations to fund these bursaries. In addition, it supports walks along Freedom Trails in Italy to commemorate the escapes by POWs and the hospitality given to them during their attempts to reach safety. The Trust also holds an annual Fontanellato luncheon in London, issues an annual newsletter, and has an archive of more than 300 books and manuscripts.

9. The Royal British Legion

Website: www.britishlegion.org.uk

10. The Second World War Experience Centre

2, Feast Field (off Town Street), Horsforth, Leeds, LS18 4TJ.
Website: www.war-experience.org

11. Associazione Nazionale Partigiani d'Italia (ANPI)

The National Association of Italian Partisans
Website: www.anpi.it

Includes details of regional and provincial branches.

12. Ministero per i beni e le Attività Culturali

Guide to Resistance and contemporary life archives:
Website: http://beniculturali.ilc.cnr.it/insmli

13. Italian Ministry of Defence

Website: www.difesa.it

14. Magazines

a. *Ancestors* magazine
www.ancestorsmagazine.co.uk

b. *Britain at War Magazine*
www.britain-at-war-magazine.com

c. *Family Tree Magazine,* and *Practical Family History*
www.family-tree.co.uk

d. *Military History,* and *World War II*
www.historynet.com

c. *Military Illustrated*
www.adhpublishing.com

f. *The Wartime News*
www.wartimenews.co.uk

Bibliography

Aimi, Amos, and Copelli, Aldo, *Fidenza Nella Resistenza*, Fidenza: Collana Storica Fidentina, 1984.

Billany, Dan, in collaboration with Dowie, David, *The Cage*, London: Longmans, 1949.

Churchill, Winston S, *The Second World War, Volume V, Closing the Ring*, London: Book Club Associates, 1987.

Comyn, John, *Episodes*, private circulation, 1994.

Davies, Tony, *When the Moon Rises*, London: Sphere Books, 1988.

De Burgh, Hugo, *Oldtown, the House and its People*, privately published, 2007.

English, Ian, ed., *Home by Christmas?* Privately published, 1997.

Foot, Michael, and Langley, James, *MI 9, Escape and Evasion 1939-1945*, London: Book Club Associates, 1979.

Gilbert, Michael, *Death in Captivity*, London: Hamlyn, 1985.

Graham, Dominick, *The Escapes and Evasions of 'An Obstinate Bastard,'* York: Wilton 65, 2000.

Hood, Stuart, *Carlino*, Manchester: Carcanet Press, 1985.

Kindersley, Philip, The Hon., *For You the War is Over*, Tunbridge Wells: Midas Books, 1983.

Lamb, Richard, *War in Italy 1943-1945, A Brutal Story*, London: Penguin, 1995.

Langrishe, John, *The Long Walk Out, or Home for Christmas*, private circulation, 1994.

La Rosa, Anna, *Storia della Resistenza nel Piacentino*, Piacenza: Amministrazione Provinciale, 1985.

Lett, Gordon, *Rossano, An Adventure of the Italian Resistance*, republished by Brian Gordon Lett, 2001.

Mather, Carol, *When the Grass Stops Growing, A War Memoir*, Barnsley: Leo Cooper, 1999.

Minardi, Marco, *L' Orizzonte del Campo*, Fidenza: Casa Editrice Mattioli, 1995.

Newby, Eric, *Love and War in the Apennines*, London: Pan Books, 1983.

Newby, Wanda, *Peace and War, Growing up in Fascist Italy*, London: Collins, 1991.

Prati, Giuseppe, *La Resistenza in Val d'Arda*, Piacenza: Casa Editrice Vicolo del Pavone, 1994.

Procacci, Giuliano, *History of the Italian People*, Harmondsworth: Penguin, 1986.

Ross, Michael, *From Liguria with Love*, London: Minerva Press, 1997.

Scaglioni, Oreste, *Memorie di vita Partigiana fra la Val Ceno e la Valdarda*, private circulation, n.d.

Scaglioni, Oreste, *Rime sulla Val d'Arda Partigiana*, private circulation, n.d.

Simpson, William, *A Vatican Lifeline '44*, London: Leo Cooper, 1995.

Tudor, Malcolm, *At War in Italy 1943-1945, True Adventures in Enemy Territory*, Newtown: Emilia Publishing, 2007.

Tudor, Malcolm, *British Prisoners of War in Italy: Paths to Freedom*, Newtown: Emilia Publishing, 2000.

Tudor, Malcolm, *Escape from Italy, 1943-45, Allied Escapers and Helpers in Fascist Italy*, Newtown: Emilia Publishing, 2003.

Tudor, Malcolm, *Prisoners and Partisans: Escape and Evasion in World War II Italy*, Newtown: Emilia Publishing, 2006.

Tudor, Malcolm, *Special Force: SOE and the Italian Resistance 1943-1945*, Newtown: Emilia Publishing, 2004.

Index of Names

Avio PG113 (Trento)

Pecorano cheese
from Goats milk